SURVEY OF RESEARCH IN POLITICAL SCIENCE ON NORTH EAST INDIA (1970–1990)

L.S. Gassah

Regency Publications
New Delhi

ISBN 81-86030-91-3

Published by Regency Publications, 20/36-G, Old Market, West Patel Nagar, New Delhi 110 008 for Indian Council of Social Science Research — North-Eastern Regional Centre, Shillong, and Printed at Radiant Printers, New Delhi 110 008, Phones: 571 2539, 574 0038; Telefax: 578 3571.

Foreword

The Advisory Committee of the NERC-ICSSR at its meeting held on November 22, 1991 decided to review the literature on North East India in the academic disciplines of Economics, Geography, History, Political Science and Sociology during the period 1970–1990, and sponsor the projects. Consequently scholars in these fields were identified and the work was entrusted to them. Most of the scholars who were entrusted to review the literature in their subjects have either completed their work or are in the process of completing it soon. We are, therefore, in a position now to publish these reviews one by one.

Review of published literature on North East India in Political Science was entrusted to Professor L.S. Gassah, of the Department of Political Science, North Eastern Hill University, Shillong. Professor Gassah has taught the subject for a number of years and has published a number of books and articles. He makes full use of his wide teaching and research experience in this review of literature in Political Science.

Political Science as we study and understand it today is primarily an academic discipline of Western origin. India also developed a branch of study known as *dandaniti* quite early. *Arthasastra of Kautilya* is too well known a work on the subject. A number of works of the subject were written in later periods also. Most Political Science Departments have a paper of Ancient Indian Political thought in their Syllabi. This area of study has been occasionally studied by political scientists. This area of study is now being taken up mostly by historians and is usually studied on Western lines.

A work of this kind requires the cooperation of a number of scholars in the field as well as adequate resources. North East India is an extensive region having its own problems and difficulties. Keeping all these in view the review of literature was limited to publications in English alone. Professor Gassah has tried to collect all the available publications in English in this work and has made it as complete and comprehensive as possible.

We take this opportunity to thank him for his painstaking work and for cooperating with the NERC-ICSSR, Shillong.

We are glad to offer this work to the general public and the students and scholars interested in the study of different aspects of the literature developed on Political Science on North East India during 1970–1990, not only within this region but also outside, and hope that it will be useful both to students and scholars alike.

Jai Prakash Singh
Honorary Director

Preface

This book *Survey of Research in Political Science on North East India* (1970–1990), is the result of the Project assigned to me by the Indian Council of Social Science Research, North-Eastern Regional Centre, Shillong. The objective behind this whole exercise is to review the literature in Political Science published in English either in the form of a book or printed articles published in different Journals about the North-Eastern Region during the period of twenty years (1970–1990). The period of twenty years is indeed very vast to cover the whole field of literature in Political Science in North East India. However, this humble, timely and earnest exercise in trying to give such a review has brought some of the least known pieces of literature in the concerned discipline to light and provided ready references to those who are interested in this field of study.

The 1960s proved to be eventful years of political movements in North-East India. The movements veered round the demand for more political autonomy to the hill people of the region which later culminated with the creation/formation/establishment of separate hill States in the region beginning with Nagaland as a full-fledged State in December 1963. Autonomous District Councils under the Sixth Schedule to the Constitution of India were however in existence since 1952 in certain hill districts of the then composite State of Assam.

The demand for separate hill States gave rise to a number of proposals, plans, suggestions, etc., which were offered to the hill people from time to time to meet their demands for both administrative and political structures in different shades and forms. Against this background of the hill State movements, one would also expect a rise and an increase in literature concerning politics and political development — both constitutional and administrative. This expectation did take a serious turn and systematic analysis of the political situation that took shape during that time had an immense impact in the later years.

Some of the literature on Political Science *per se* as a discipline did not take place immediately. Very few books which may be said to cater to the needs and understanding of the discipline of Political Science did not find an appreciable place even in the later part of the 1960s. However, many teachers and researchers belonging especially to the disciplines of Political Science and History, both at the College and University levels, did make use of the situations prevailing in the 1960s as starting points, because this period offered them immense background materials to analyse the later political developments in the region. Therefore, a decade later, saw a number of printed materials in the form of books, journals, magazines, proceedings of seminars and newspaper reports which have really enriched the discipline of Political Science. This kind of academic exercise brings the whole of North East India into focus and limelight even outside its own geographical boundaries. The increase number of literature on such studies of political development of the region also brings more understanding about the political situation and reality that takes place not only among the Political Scientists of the region but outside also. It gives way to attract more attention of the experts in the discipline by way of their interaction with the local scholars or their comments on what was happening in the region. Against this background, the review of the two decades (1970–1990) of literature in Political Science with special reference to the North Eastern region makes it interesting and worthwhile as far as the discipline is concerned.

The present exercise is a humble one — and by no means complete. However, a beginning is made in trying to unearth the literature in Political Science with a North East perspective.

I would like to offer my sincere thanks to the Chairman, the Honorary Director and the Deputy Director of ICSSR (NERC), Shillong for this task assigned to me and to Regency Publications, New Delhi for their timely publication of the Volume.

L.S. Gassah

Contents

Introduction

Political Science as an independent discipline among other Social Science disciplines has already gained an important status especially in the field of teaching in all North East India Universities. It is very encouraging to see that Political Science is one of the most popular subjects taught both at the under-graduate and post-graduate levels; the subject is even taught at the higher secondary school level but under a different subject matter. More encouraging in this respect is to find that all colleges with Arts stream have Political Science Departments. So also at the University or post-graduate level. To this effect, the UGC panel in its report entitled, *Political Science in India: State of the Discipline and Agenda for the Future* (1982), stated clearly that Political Science in India is a very popular discipline with the students at the under-graduate as well as post-graduate levels; even its M.Phil courses have begun to attract a number larger than what policy-makers visualised only a couple of years ago. In quantitative terms at least, the discipline can be regarded as having consolidated itself in the mainstream of Indian academic life. However, the report did not hesitate to state that this phenomenon of popularity is because of the general feeling among the students that Political Science is one of the easier disciplines to pass.[1] This is also true in particular with the students of the North Eastern Universities.

---

1. Narain, Iqbal and Mathur, P.C. *Political Science in India: State of the Discipline and Agenda for the Future,* UGC, New Delhi, 1982, p. 5.

But as far as 'research' strictly or directly dealing with Political Science is concerned, much area is still left to be empirically covered by researchers interested in the discipline. This is because of the fact that some research works submitted to different Departments of Political Science in the Universities of the North East do not have direct bearing of the discipline *per se*. This is because of the importance being given to inter or multidisciplinary approach. Thus it is opined that during the last three decades in the name of research in the discipline of Political Science, a few monographs came out from the Universities of North East India which have meaning in their respective fields and each of which reports and states the fact about the particular situation but the general relationship of these studies have yet to be rigorously pursued.[2]

Political Science is, at the global level, an intellectual discipline of great antiquity. Poitical Science, along with a host of other disciplines, made its appearance on the Indian scene only in the twentieth century and the history of its separate development in independent university teaching department spans less than half a dozen decades.[3]

Political Science began in the United States of America. In this sense it has become a western discipline which has come to occupy an important position in academics all over the world. Prior to the emergence of this western discipline, there were attempts at understanding state craft and also reflections on what could be called political philosophy. But systematic study of politics as a profession had never been taken seriously. Emergence of Political Science marked an interest in what is called 'real politics'.[4] Political Science studies in Indian universities originated, generally speaking, under the institutional auspices of History departments, both at the level of teaching and research. In some universities, however,

2. Ray, B. Datta, The Status of Research in Political Science in North East India: Some Observations, *Journal of NEICSSR*, Vol. 14, No. 2, October 1990, p. 53
3. Narain and Mathur, *op. cit.*, p. 1.
4. Baruah, A.K., Mainstream Political Science and its Pitfalls, *Proceedings of the North East India Political Science Association* (hereafter NEIPSA Proceedings), Second Annual Conference, Guwahati, 1992, p. 44.

Political Science courses formed an integral part of Economics curricula, while in others Philosophy occupied a dominant position in relation to Political Science courses. In strict theory, such a situation, could have conceivable led to cross-fertilization of Political Science studies by insights drawn from such sister disciplines as History, Economics and Philosophy. However, in actual practice the subordination of Political Science to other disciplins, not only retarded its growth, but also prevented the students from taking advantage of latest developments in teaching and research which are taking place in the discipline all over the world, particularly after the mid-forties.[5] The North East experience came much later this period as we shall see in the following paragraphs.

The UGC Panel Report (1982) in its analysis of the 'state of the discipline' (Political Science) further found that, in a very fundamental sense a discipline like Political Science with its emphasis on a tradition of free and frank enquiry into political issues can prosper only after a country has attained independence. It is, therefore, not surprising that the emphasis in pre-independent India remained largely confined to the study of political classics, political history and constitutions. Beyond this foci, Political Science studies and also a large number of research institutes received a fillip only after India attained independence in 1947.[6] In the case of North East India, the position and status of Political Science in teaching and research came much later even from the Indian standard point of view. It took more than ten years even after the establishment of the first University in the region in 1948 at Guwahati that the first batch of Political Scientists came out successfully in 1961. Before that period, students desiring to study Political Science had to opt for Political Science group in Economics, both at the under-graduate and post-graduate levels. But during the last more than thirty years, the number of Political Scientists is gradually increasing with the increase in the number of Universities in the North Eastern region. In fact, it is the most popular course of study among students in the

5. Narain and Mathur, *op. cit.*, p. 1.
6. *Ibid.*, p. 5.

faculty of Social Sciences.[7] The response of students was so good that sometimes it becomes a problem to accommodate or admit all those who seek admission at the post-graduate level.

Gauhati University being the oldest University in the North Eastern region took the lead in respect of giving certain status to the discipline even though at the initial stage, the University which was started in 1948, came to have a separate Department of Political Science ten years after that, that is, in 1958. From then on, there was no looking back. Political Science as an independent discipline has made rapid strides and faster development and therefore attained an unparallel weight and status in terms of its importance, significance, prominence and popularity among the teachers and students of the North Eastern region. In many Colleges and Universities of the regon, its popularity can be easily judged from the number of students intake, being the most sought after discipline both at the under and post-graduate levels.

In 1966, another University in Assam was established, that is, Dibrugarh University with Political Science as one of the Departments; next followed the J.N.U. Centre at Imphal (now Manipur University) which also has the department of Political Science.

The North Eastern Hill University was established by an Act of Parliament in 1973. But Political Science Department of this University was started only in 1974 with few students. But since 1975, the number of students intake of the Department increased rapidly. NEHU being a Central University, attracted a lare number of students from all over the North Eastern region and even outside. As stated earlier, Political Science is one of the most popular disciplines among the students at the under-graduate level. The same popularity is also experienced at the post-graduate level of all the Universities in the region that have the Department of Political Science.

As far as teaching of the discipline like Political Science is concerned, there are few limitations that both the teachers

---

7. Pakem, B., North East India Political Science Association: Presidential Address, *NEIPSA Proceedings*, Second Annual Conference, Guwahati, 1992, p. 2.

and the taught are facing in this part of the country. One of the limitations that can be pointed out here is due to the lack of reading materials especially in those areas that concerned with up-to-date information. The Colleges and Universities in North East India being located in such a remote and far off region of the Indian Union, coupled with communication bottlenecks and other related difficulties, put the educational institutions, the students and the teachers in great difficulty. Reading and other library facilities which are easily available in other parts of the country cannot be said to be sufficiently available or within an easy reach of the teachers and students of the North Eastern Universities and other educational institutions. Against this background, it may be stated that teaching of Political Science has been affected seriously due to lack of reading materials. The situation is more acute in the case of colleges at the rural or interior places. Sometimes even after the Political Science syllabi have been revised and updated, yet reading materials are out of reach of both the teachers and students.

In 1974,[8] the North Eastern Hill University with the financial assistance of the Indian Council for Social Science Research through its Eastern Regional Centre, Calcutta, had organised a workshop in St. Edmund's College, Shillong, "to involve Social Science teachers in the Contemporary Methodology of their discipline to help them to relate their teaching to regional needs of production, and development and to be aware of the need for constant syllabus revision in the light of socio-economic and other changes as knowledge increases." In a section on Political Science teaching and research, it was observed that India and for that matter in North Eastern India, teaching and research in the discipline was "vitiated by theoretical assumptions, currently fashionable in the U.S. and European literature, based on anthropological theories of structural-functionalism which looked at political life as a static condition and not as a dynamic process, continually subject to change." Further, it was also pointed out that "Political Science should be taught as the means of power for social progress."

8. Pakem, B. *op.cit.*, p. 1.

The history of research in Political Science in the North Eastern region is of very recent origin. The reason for starting this important aspect late is obvious. As stated earlier, the first University in the region, Gauhati University, was started only in 1948. At the level of research, it was only in 1967, that the first doctorate degree in Political Science was conferred on a research scholar whose field of study was more relevant to Economics. Later on, the M.Phil and Ph.D research degrees were also conferred on a number of research scholars in the region. In addition to these, there are also teachers and other research students who had undertaken research works in the field of Political Science who did not work for a research degree. Such research papers produced by research scholars of North East India cover topics on local, regional, national and international issues.[9] A further analysis of these researches conducted both at the University departments and outside point out to the various and varied research activities in the field of Administration-Educational, Jail, Municipal, Revenue, Personnel, University, Secretariat, British-Relations with North East India, Centre-State Relations, Inter-State Relations; Community Developments, Rural Development Programmes and Panchayats; Electoral Studies, Voting Behaviour; Federalism, Regionalism; International Relations — Indo-British, Indo-Burmese, Indo-Sri Lanka, Indo-Bangladesh, Indo-Pak and International Politics; Legislative Assembly, Local Self-Government, Political Development and Change, Modern and Traditional Leadership, Elite studies, Middle class, Political Parties, Political and Social Change, Public Service Commission; Sixth Schedule, Governor, Deputy Commissioner, Traditional Institutions, Social and Cultural Life, State Politics, Urban Politics, Students' Movements and Politics, Ethnicity and a host of other political problems and issues. But we have yet to have standard research works in the field of Political Theory which is an important aspect of Political studies.[10]

On the question of appraisal of research on Political Science in North East India, it may be said that no appraisal of the extent and nature of such research has ever been made so

9. *Ibid.*, p. 2.
10. Pakem, B., *op.cit.*, p. 4.

far. It is only after a proper survey of the research materials on the discipline and summaries of the same are made that a critical appraisal of research in Political Science in North East India can be done.[11] There is also the problem of the lack of knowledge and co-ordination among various University's departments in the region itself. This gives rise even to the problem of the research students doing research on the same topic in more than two University Political Science Departments. This is because no one knows what others are doing in their research works. This should not have happened had there been an exchange of idea and information among the various Political Science departments of different Universities and other research institutions in the region. It is high time therefore among the various University Political Science departments and other research institutions in the region in order to avoid duplication of doing research on the same topic(s) as well as to know who works on what problems or issues. This will also help to enrich the discipline especially in terms of research. Perhaps because of this fact, it led to the formation of such associations like the former Assam Political Science Association (APSA) and the present North East India Political Science Association (NEIPSA). The advantage of forming such associations is to bring together during the Annual Conferences all those Political Science teachers, students and others who are interested in political studies into a common platform where they can share and discuss the common problems and issues confronting them. Against this background, therefore, the Second Annual Conference of NEIPSA held under the auspices of the premier University in the region, that is, Gauhati University in 1992 that the organisers felt it is urgently necessary to discuss an important issue on *The Status of teaching and research of Political Science in North East India*. The result of this exercise is immensely fruitful. Thus in the Proceedings of NEIPSA published after the end of that Conference, there are as many as 5(five) research papers on the above theme. This shows the anxiety and concern of the Political Scientists of the region towards the discipline both in terms of the problem of teaching and its status in research.

11. *Ibid.*

This is a very welcome trend set in the right direction. Serious discussions of this nature in the near future may also be able to bring to light many other important aspects of Political Science studies in the region.

The 1960s proved to be eventful years of political movements in North-East India. The movements veered round the demand for more political autonomy to the hill people of the region which later culminated with the creation/formation/establishment of separate hill States in the region beginning with Nagaland as a full-fledged State in December 1963. Autonomous District Councils (ADCs) under the Sixth Schedule to the Constitution were however in existence since 1952 in certain hill districts of the then composite State of Assam. Before the reorganisation of Assam, the hill leaders have had a second look for scrutiny of the initial autonomy granted to them through the Autonomous District Councils and found that such constitutional arrangement was inadequate. The hill leaders even in 1954 were of the opinion that 'autonomy' under the Sixth Schedule to the Constitution was not a 'real autonomy' as per the resolution passed by the Chief Executive Members in their conference held at Tura in 1954. Thus, besides the demand for the amendment of the Sixth Schedule, an added dimension was given to the demand for separate hill States for the autonomous districts, tll then under the composite State of Assam.

The demand for separate hill States led to the appointment of different committees, sub-committees and commissions to examine and study the varied demands of the hill people in North East India. This gave rise to a number of proposals, plans, suggestions, etc. which were offered to the hill people from time to time to meet their demands for both administrative and political structures in different shades and forms

Against this background of the hill State movements, one would also expect a rise and an increase in literature concerning politics and political development — both constitutional and administrative. This expectation did take a serious turn and systematic analysis of the political situation that took shape during that time had an immense impact in the later years.

But some of the literature on Politial Science *per se* as a discipline did not take place immediately. Very few books which may be said to cater to the needs and understanding of the discipline of Political Science did not find an appreciable place even in the later part of the 1960s. However, many teachers and researchers belonging especially to the disciplines of Political Science and History, both at the College and University levels, did make use of the situations prevailing in the 1960s as starting points, because this period offered them immense background materials to analyse the later political developments in the region. Therefore, a decade later, saw a number of printed materials in the form of books, journals, magazines, proceedings of seminars and newspaper reports which have really enriched the discipline of Political Science. This kind of academic exercise brings the whole of North East India into focus and limelight even outside its own geographical boundaries. The increase number of literature on such studies of political development of the region also brings more understanding about the political situation and reality that takes place not only among the political scientists of the region but outside also. It gives way to attract more attention of the experts in the discipline by way of their interaction with the local scholars or their comments on what was happening in the region. Against this background, the review/ survey of the two decades (1970–1990) of liteature in Political Science with special reference to the North Eastern region makes it interesting and worthwhile as far as the discipline is concerned.

The present exercise is a humble one — and by no means complete. However, a beginning is made in trying to unearth the literature in Political Science with a North-East perspective.

Literature on General Problems/ Issues of North-East India

It is interesting to note the presence and availability of literature discussing the general political problems and issues of N.E. India. Some such books are edited volumes. They are actually the outcome of Seminars, Conferences, Symposia, etc., held by different research organisations and institutions, mostly involved on research activities on the problems of N.E. India. A number of interesting topics could be found in such edited volumes covering different disciplines (mostly Social Sciences). While reviewing these literature, an attempt is made to sift them carefully in order to extract information relating to Political Science. Wherever necessary the articles which could be said to have contributed to enrich understanding of political problems and issues are listed in the review. This makes it easier for those who go through this report to find out specific articles in a particular book(s) as reference source(s). However, some of these articles may not be on Political Science *per se* but at least they are falling under the applied side of the discipline.

A cursory examination of these books will show that they cover a wide canvass of political problems and issues relating to N.E. India.

One interesting aspect of these books is the analytical framework provided to understand the social and political significance of the traditional institutions prevailing among the people of N.E. India of the causes/factors responsible for the abolition of the same. Where these traditional institutions are still in existence, an attempt is also made to analyse the situation in their relations with the modern constitutional setup or institutions. Two things could be derived here: One, the probem of conflict between tradition and modernity or in other sense, the tradition-modernity dichotomy, and secondly, the co-existence between the two institutions in spite of certain problems.

Some of these books are based strictly on the historical and constitutional development of N.E. India since the British period. Therefore, we find few scholars both from the disciplines of Political Science and History who made serious attempts to place those documents as they are with their comments and still others tried to analyse the contents of the documents in order to understand the political situation of N.E. India both during the British period and after that. These books become very important reference materials on which a scholar who is interested to study the political dimensions of N.E. India has to consult them.

Broadly speaking, the third common dimension that may be pinpointed here about these books is the basic information that they try to bring out on certain sensitive issues and problems that may be said to have shaken even the feeling of "Indianness" to put it bluntly. Therefore, such basic fundamental questions like 'nationalism', 'regionalism', 'nationality', 'identity', 'social and political tension', and such other crises of the twentieth century N.E. India have been discussed by many prominent figures in these books, keeping in view the data which come from North-East India.

The book *Problem of the Hil Tribes: N.E. Frontier (1822–42)* Vol. I by H.K. Barpujari (1970) is an appraisal of the problem of the hill tribes of North East Frontier in its early phase. The factors and forces at work in moulding the British policy towards these tribes are analysed and examined in this volume. The book has given an analysis of the political situation in North-East India in the early phase of the British administration. Though historical in its approach, the book contains an enormous piece of information relating to Britih contact with the Hill Tribes of the frontier region and the type of administrative acumen introduced by them.

The book *David Scott in North-East India (1802–1831)* by Nirode K. Barooah (1970) though written on and about David Scott, who stands out, undoubtedly, as one of the most fascinating civil servants of the East India Company, provides immense sources of information of British paternalism in N.E. India (as suggests in the sub-title). This dominant feature of Scott's ideas of administration was expressly described by the author in the first chapter itself. The last chapter, while making some concluding remarks on Scott's philosophy of government, tries to describe what types of paternalism it was. The chapters in between deal with some of the important subjects that the British paternalists in India were most concerned with in the early nineteenth century. The book gives us some insights of historical facts of the British policy in general and David Scott's in particular, in dealing with N.E. India. The book unfolds interesting administrative and political policies and development during the time of David Scott. The encounters of the people against the British policy of annexation, make it more interesting for further analytial assessment of the situation that prevailed at that period of history of the region.

The book *Hill Politics in North-East India* by Shibanikinkar Chaube (1973) is one of the most oft quoted books on northeast politics as it happens to be one such earliest attempt to study the politics and political development in the region scientifically. The author expresses that the primary purpose of the book is to present the maximum amount of 'facts' that one could gather about a problem region of India. He is also of the opinon that there is lack of understanding, in the rest of the country, of the political turmoil in N.E. India. The argument of this volume is that the 'tribal' situation in N.E. India cannot be properly understood except by viewing it in its historical perspective. Although the method of this study is basically political, the author has made use of history, geography and sociology. The book is recognised as an authoritative volume on the political issues and development of N.E. India. It also covers a wide canvas in its universe by analysing most of the political problems of all the political units of N.E. India. The book is an indispensable source of information and reference and therefore enriched to a great extent literature on Political Science.

As mentioned in the Introduction, the book *The Challenge of the North-East* by Sudhakar Bhat (1975) is one of the earliest books which tries to discuss and analyse the various administrative and political problems of N.E. India following the scheme of its re-organisation. Except Nagaland, the author tried to analyse the political developments in N.E. India taking into account a particular aspect, that is, Christianity and its role in North-East politics besides other issues. The book was also written while such areas like Mizoram and Arunachal Pradesh were still Union Territories. The author tried to bring some of the challenges that N.E. India was facing earlier and how these aspects have led to many problems in the region.

The book *A Statistical Account of Assam*, Vol. II by W.W. Hunter (1975: Reprint) was first published in 1879. This volume consists of ethno, cultural and administrative accounts of the districts of Goalpara (including the Eastern Dwars), the Garo Hills, the Naga Hills, the Khasi and Jaintia Hills, Sylhet and Cachar. The book will be of great help to students and teachers of Political Science especially those chapters dealing with administrative accounts of the districts mentioned above. The book provides background materials on the early administrative development during the British period and the relations between the people of those districts with the British administration. The book forms an important source of reference on the earlier administrative history of certain districts of North-East India.

In March, 1975, the Department of Political Science, Dibrugarh University held a three-day National Seminar on "Political Development in North-East India". The Seminar elaborately discussed various aspects of political development in the North-Eastern region. A total of thirteen papers besides the inaugural addresses by the V.C. Dibrugarh University and the former Chief Minister of Assam were published in two volumes entitled *Political Development in North East India* edited by T.C. Bose (1976 & 1978). In the issue published in 1976, the volume included mainly articles on Arunachal Pradesh. These articles discussed in great details about the political and administrative development in Arunachal

Pradesh. The articles therefore contributed a lot to the understanding of the political situation in that State. The other volume which was published in 1978 included the other papers presented in the Seminar (1975) on various aspects of political development in N.E. India. These articles dealt with general problems and issues concerning N.E. India and other States, with special reference to case studies on Assam, Meghalaya and Mizoram. As the articles on this volume discussed both the general and particular issues and problems of N.E. India, they therefore brought into focus a wide canvas of interests on the overall political and administrative developments in N.E. India.

A Century of Tribal Politics in North East India (1874–1974) by V. Venkata Rao (1976) is one of the most oft quoted books on North East politics by students of Political Science and others who are interested in the political development and issues concerning North East India. The book is an indepth study of tribal politics in North East India from 1874–1974. The contents of the book are divided into three parts. Part I discusses a profile of N.E. India, political development, relations between the tribals and the British, constitutional position and tribal political systems. Part II is fully dedicated on the discussion relating to the District Councils — their structure, membership, functions and working, and Part III is concerned with State Politics — where formation of States in N.E. India was discussed beginning with the formation of the State of Nagaland (1963). Other chapters included here are that of elections to the Legislature, Regional Political Parties and formation of governments in different States of the region. The book provides immense source materials on tribal politics in N.E. India. It enriches and contributes immensely to the literature on Political Science in N.E. India and therefore becomes an indispensable source of information.

The book *Problem of the Hill Tribes: N.E. Frontier (1843–1872)* by H.K. Barpujari (1978) traces the development of British policy towards the N.E. Frontier tribes during the period 1842 to 1872. The forces and factors that led to the changes in policy — from non-interference to total involvement and annexation adopted by the British towards the hill tribes are analysed and examined by the author in their proper perspective. The problem of the frontier defence and the evolution of the administrative structure of the tribal areas according to the needs and circumstances are also discussed in this volume. The book is mainly based on unpublished documents. Though the author's approach is from the historical point of view, the book provides immense resource materials for students of Political Science also. The book unfolds an interesting political and administrative development under the British administration in their relationship with the frontier areas and people of N.E. India.

The author of the book *Historical and Constitutional Documents of North-Eastern India (1824–1973)*, Manilal Bose (1979) tries to put together through this book, a large number of official documents to construct the historical and political development of N.E. India beginning with the Treaty of Yandabo of 1826. These archival documents are of vital importance. The documents have been compiled and classified into four parts beginning with the Treaty of Yandabo 1826. An attempt has also been made to show the evolution of the administration of the North-East Frontier Agency (NEFA) and the break up of North-Eastern India into several States. Relevant Regulations, Orders, Acts and Constitutional Provisions relating to N.E. India have been included in this pioneering archival compilation. The book may be of great help to students of Political Science as it offers them those various types of documents for ready reference. These documents help when put to analysis to understand the minds, the ideas and plans of the decision-makers. Sometimes, the original documents are not easily available to readers; this compilation makes them available. In order to understand the political developments of the North Eastern region, these documents have to be taken seriously. The British relations with the people and their chiefs could be gleaned through the different agreements signed. Such agreements are included in this book. The modern political history of N.E. India is flooded with a number of Acts, Rules and Regulations passed from time to time by the Government of India; these are also provided in the book. Students of Political Science who want to have a first hand knowledge of these Acts, Rules, Regulations etc. will find this book to be of great help.

Alexander Mackenzie's *The North-East Frontier of India* (reprint 1979) is a new title of the earlier one. This book is often quoted by teachers and students of Social Sciences. It gives detailed information about the British relations with the people of Assam and especially the people of the hills of N.E. India. Mackenzie has made a general survey of the political relations of the British Government of India with the hill tribes of Assam, Cachar and Chittagong which proved extremely useful to the local administration as well as to the foreign department of the then British Indian Government. The book provides rich materials on the North-Eastern region which no serious scholar can afford to ignore. Part I of the book deals with Sub-Himalayan region from Bhutan to Arunachal Pradesh. Part II and III give a graphic account of the dealings of the British Government with the tribes to the south of the Brahmaputra and Surma valleys and to the Chittagong Hill Tracts. The conclusions and observations drawn by the author are of absorbing interest. The book is an indispensable reference source to students of Political Science as it provides detailed information of the political development in North-East India during the British rule.

The Fifth and Sixth Schedules to the Constitution of India by M. Hidayatullah (1979) is the outcome of the Anundoram Borooah Law Lectures delivered by the author in November 1978. The original topic of the lectures was "the Scope and Application of the Provisions of the Fifth and Sixth Schedules of the Constitution of India". Until the time the lectures were delivered, this area of study was not academically fully explored. However, Justice Hidayatullah has lucidly analysed and interpreted the provisios of the Fifth and Sixth Schedules so as to remove the complexities and make them intelligible even to a lay reader. These lectures published in the present form of the book contain three main topics — (1) Mainly Historical, (2) Constitutional Making, and (3) the Experience. This book containing the lectures will be of immense practical use to the administrators of the country, particularly of the North-Eastern region. Students of Political Science will also find the book to be of great benefit especially those who are interested in the constitutional history, working and functioning of these two important schedules which are made applicable to certain areas of N.E. India.

The book *India's North-East In Flames* by V.I.K. Sarin (1980), is one of the earlier attempts to discuss and analyse the complexity of insurgent movements confronting the seven political units of N.E. India. The book stresses the geopolitical significance of this sensitive region and describes how various foreign powers are trying to make it a cockpit of international intrigues. The author also examines the explosive problem of infiltration of foreign nationals as well as inter-State migrants into the North Eastern States and how this problem assumes social, economic, culture and communal overtones. To overcome these problems the author has put forward some suggestions to bring peace and understanding in a trouble torn North-Eastern region. The book makes an interesting study on the background of insurgency in N.E. India and the involvement of many forces behind this knotty question which has been haunting the minds of the people of North-East India.

H.K. Sareen's *Insurgency in North-East India (A Study of Sino-American Role)* was published in 1980. An attempt has been made by the author in this book to trace in detail the evolution of the insurgency movement in North-East India with special attention given to the Sino-American role. The policy of the erstwhile British rulers was to keep the tribes of the region as far removed from the mainstream of national life as possible and they were thus isolated and left to themselves. Taking advantage of these people, foreign elements with local Maoist support hatched a conspiracy to foment discontent and encourage secessionist tendencies. Thus, they posed a grave danger to the security of the region and the integrity of the Indian Union in general. The author attempts to analyse the involvement of the Peoples Republic of China in fomenting the insurgecy movement which started in Nagaland and spread to other States of N.E. India, especially Mizoram and Manipur. In the same way, the author tries to probe into the involvement of the CIA in the secessionist movement. The role of both these foreign elements has been brought in the pages of the book. Though journalistic in approach, the book thus provides another picture of the problem of insurgency in N.E. India and the role played by outside agencies.

The book *British Relations with the Hill Tribes of Assam since 1858* by Birendra Ch. Chakravorty (1981), as its title suggests, deals with the British relations with the hill tribes of N.E. India since 1858. Though the author's approach is mostly from the historical persective, the book, however, provides materials which may be of help to the discipline of Political Science. The author also quoted extensively the official letters and documents available in the annals of the British records. These documents form an important source and reference materials for better understanding and analysis of the administrative and political relationship between the British and the political units in N.E. India during the British rule.

H.K. Barpujari, a renowned historian of North-East India has given to the readers the volume (Vol. III) entitled *Problem of the Hill Tribes North-East Frontier 1873–1962*, published in 1981, covering such a vast canvas from Inner Line to McMahon Line. The book deals mainly with the tribes which remained unsubdued or beyond the pale of British influence till the closing years of the last century. The author opens his discussion with the boundary disputes with the Nagas which continue to plague even now the relations with their neighbours in the plains. As a panacea followed the Inner Line which sought to debar over-zealous officers, except under compelling circumstances, from meddling into affairs of the tribal people. The author tried to answer some of the pertinent questions of the changes of British policy towards the tribal people and the causes and factors which led the British to adopt a forward policy. The author not only unfolds the establishment of British paramountcy over the tribes that stubbornly resisted till the end, but also comes out with the main trends and development in NEFA, the evolution of the McMahon Line and the subsequent border dispute with China. Based mainly on primary sources, this volume contributes a lot to understanding of administrative and political development in N.E. India during the period under study.

The edited volume by J.B. Bhattacharjee on *Social Tension in North-East India* (1982) has emerged in a book form out of the papers presented in a colloquium organised by the North-

East India Council for Social Science Research (NEICSSR), Shillong, in 1980. The North-Eastern region of India has been passing through prolonged social tensions ever since the agitation for the detection and deportation of foreign nationals in Assam and this has its effect on other States of N.E. India too. The volume is an attempt made by the academicians, journalists, public men, admnistrators and social workers drawn from the region's population to study the origin and magnitude of the problem and suggest possible solutions. The volume presents to the readers those conflicting and divergent views and findings at a time when in the best interest of the nation, the intellectuals have to find a way out to ease the charged situation in the North-Eastern sentinel of the country. The contributors do not only analyse the social tension but some of them took the pain to analyse the political tension also in the region and this makes the book to be of interest to students of Political Science and enriched the discipline too.

'The unrest on India's North-Eastern borders has risen not from want of goodwill on anybody's part but from a failure of understanding', opines the author of the book *Imperilled Frontiers (India's North-Eastern Borderlands),* Nari Rustomji (1983). This failure to understand the varied problems of N.E. India gives rise to numerous other problems which are still lingering. India can therefore ill afford in allowing conditions of unrest and disorder to fester indefinitely on her vitally strategic north-eastern borders. Mr. Rustomji analyses in this book the causes underlying the growing unrest in N.E. India. He demonstrates very forcefully that people, however primitive, present the imposition of an alien culture and that nothing gives rise to so much anger and hostility as the threat of cultural aggression. Heavy economic investment, again, is in itself of little avail in securing the goodwill and loyalty of the people of the frontiers, any more than an excessive military presence, which creates more problems than it solves. The author's central message in this book is — that while change is imperative for a community's healthy development, the pace of change must be adjusted to the community's capacity to absorb it without detriment to essential values. The book provides an interesting analysis of some of the knotty issues and problems of North-East India as a whole. The suggestions put forward by the author are of immense importance to the decision-makers dealing with the North Eastern affairs.

The collection of papers on *The Emergence and Role of Middle Class in N.E. India* (1983) edited by B. Datta Ray, is the outcome of a Seminar under the same theme in 1978. Middle Class is one of the current themes hotly debated by Social Scientists. The book therefore intends to generate a discussion on the middle class in N.E. India. Persons belonging to this class in their respective societies could be said to have emerged in N.E. India also. In the hill societies of N.E. India, middle class is said to have emerged as a result of Western education, moneytised economy and Christianity. The papers and the opinions given by the authors show that the middle class in the hills could not remain entirely out of touch with the middle class among the plains people as by that time, better contacts were established between the hills and the plains of N.E. India. In these papers some authors have taken an academically accepted definition while others based their discussion on the Marxist interpretation of class. The papers containing in this volume show a wide range of foci. One of the papers deals mainly with the theoretical problem of defining middle class and their role in the society; two papers make an assessment of the middle class in N.E. India as a whole, particularly in the hill areas and the rest of the papers are more or less case studies about the history and role of middle class in N.E. India.

Sixth Schedule to the Constitution of India — A Study, by B.L. Hansaria (1983) is one of the attempts to analyse the constitutional development relating to N.E. India. The outcome after the incorporation of this particular Schedule in the Constitution was the creation of the Autonomous District Councils for the hill areas of the then composite State of Assam, except Nagaland which flatly refused to accept the Schedule. Hansaria in this book has given the historical background leading to the framing of the Sixth Schedule and discussed the subsequent amendments of the Schedule. The Schedule contains many provisions relating to the creation, power, functions, administration — legislative, executive, judicial, etc., of the Autonomous District Councils as well as the Regional Councils subsequently. These provisions have also been analysed by the author. A critical analysis of the delicate role of the Governor in the administration of the Sixth Schedule areas was also included as one of the chapters. The last chapter deals with the Khasi States and Shillong. Detailed appendices are also given in the book regarding the Acts, Rules, Regulations, Notifications, etc. pertaining to the hill areas administration. The book provides immense detailed information on the Sixth Schedule and the administration of the Autonomous District Councils. An additional information was provided in the book with the inclusion in the Appendices on detailed discussion of the Schedule by the members of the Constituent Assembly. Students of Political Science interested in the study of the Autonomous District Councils will surely find the book very helpful.

Report on the Administration of N.E. India (1921–22), (1984), is a reprint of the earlier volume. This book gives a general discussion on the administration of N.E. India during the period under study. The period is a short one indeed but a lot of information on the earlier administration of the region by the British could be had from this book. It provides good background materials of the earlier administrative developments that took place during that period.

The book *North-East Region: Problems and Prospects of Development,* edited by B.L. Abbi (1984), is a collection of a good number of papers on the problems and prospects of development of N.E. India under the auspices of the Centre for Research in Rural and Industrial Development, Chandigarh. The authors of these various papers were drawn from diverse fields of study and disciplines, including mostly academicians, delegates representing the Assam movement on one hand, and members from the Planning Commission, diplomatic and aministrative services, industry, science and technology on the other. The experts also included eminent journalists and researchers engaged in specialised studies of the subjects.

The papers published in this volume discussed varied problems and issues relating to the main issue of the prospects of development or the hurdles/hindrances to development in N.E. India. Contributors present varied points of views but provide an insight into the nature of the problems, their magnitude and the immediate and long term prospects of development. The proceedings also reveal the dangerous consequences that lie ahead if ad-hoc descriptive diagnoses are treated as sacrosanct and accepted as possible solutions of the problems and issues pertaining to N.E. India. The book is an indispensable source of information on the problems and issues (social, economic and political) of N.E. India as a whole.

Electoral Politics in North-East India by S.K. Chaube (1985) is an attempt that has been made to record the developments up to the Seventh Lok Sabha elections in N.E. India. This volume tries to describe and analyse, the ongoing process of politics in N.E. India, the Sixth Lok Sabha elections (1977) forming its core. The author in this book has surveyed and analysed the entire gamut of the Sixth Lok Sabha elections from all the seven States of N.E. India. The book provides interesting findings on electoral political behaviour of the people of the seven States during this particular election. Students of Political Science who are interested in electoral studies will find the book to be of great help. The Appendices and tables given by the author form additional data and information.

The book *Nationalism and Regionalism in N.E. India* (Ed.) K.M. Deka (1985) is a collection of papers presented during the Seminar organised by the Department of Political Science, Dibrugarh University in 1982. The central issues of the theme of this volume are: (i) the nature and typologies of nationalism and regionalism and their relevance in the context of India, and (ii) the pattern of relationship obtaining between nationalism and regionalism, and the working of regional forces in N.E. India. The essays written by a good number of scholars mostly from N.E India itself attempt at an objective analysis of the interaction of nationalism and regionalism in N.E. India in well-balanced theoretical frameworks. The papers also provide a critique of the relevance of the existing theories of nationalism and regionalism in the Indian context. The increasing demand for more regional autonomy by the people of North East as well as the formation of more autonomos political units makes the papers presented in the book more relevant today in understanding of the background of both nationalism and regionalism.

The small booklet on *Changing North-East India*, edited by A.P. Sinha (1986) consists of three important aspects on North-East India — the Economic Condition and Change, Political Development and Change and Social Change. All the three papers are well researched and documented by the three scholars. But as far as Political Science literature is concerned, the paper by B. Pakem is most relevant. Pakem gives an extensive theoretical concept and background of political development and attempts to examine whether the same theoretical concept(s) can be made applicable to North-East India situation. In this respect, he makes use of the data and relevant information from North-East to show its peculiarities as well as its unique problems which sometimes the same theoretical concept(s) available somewhere else may or may not fit in the North-East situation. This paper contributes a lot to Political Science literature on North-East India and it becomes therefore an important reference source.

The edited volume on *Electoral Politics in N.E. India* (1986) by P.S. Datta contains twenty papers on different aspects of electoral politics and its dynamics both in the hills and plains of N.E. India. Taking the papers together, they cover a period of about four decades of electoral experiences from 1946 to 1983. The papers focus attention on the political parties (both regional and national), the participation and involvement of the electorate of N.E. India at three levels of our constitutional operation, namely, the elections to the House of the People, to the Legislative Assembly and the Autonomous District Councils.

The papers unravel the fascinating experiences of our parliamentary operation in an otherwise indifferent and (also hostile at times) soil of North East. They also document the history of transition of the system to a growing frustration towards it in the plains of North East. In short, the papers make the science of political parties or statiology an interesting area of study even in the remote North-Eastern part of the country. Moreover, as Electoral Politics and behaviour is an important constituent of political studies, the book as a whole has contributed a lot in the literature of Political Science from North East India in particular.

The Problem of Change: A Study of North-East India by B.P. Singh (1987) tries to look into the problems of North-East India from the point of view of the changes that swept the region and how this transformation has disturbed the traditional societies and the people of this far-flung north-eastern part of the country. The political and administrative arrangements in the region have also altered more drastically than in other areas. From a single composite State of Assam, six other full-fledged States come out. The ethnic variety and range of the area is the most complex in India — containing a rich variety of ethnic groups. 'Development' has in turn created opportunities and problems that have transformed the region into one of the most volatile in India. The author thus, analyses the problems and prospects of change in the region in the light of its complex history and the very major socio-economic and political developments that have occurred over the past four decades. Chapters like ethnicity, middle class, elite and regional consciousness, reorganisation of Assam, political system, administrative philosophy and institutional framework, identity crisis and economic development are to be found in the contents of the book. On the whole, the book contains a lot of information on the political development and situation in N.E. India and its analysis of the changes that took place since 1947 is thought provoking. The book has thus enriched another field of political study of the problems/issues confronting North-East India.

The book *N.E. India: Quest for Identity* by Udayon Misra (1988) is the collection of articles dealing with socio-political developments covering an important phase in the post-independence history of North-East. Though many of the articles were written as responses to developments in the contemporary scene, they are marked by a deep sense of introspection. The struggle of the different nationalities particularly that of the Assamese and the Nagas, had been dealt with by the author. The author's insight into the problems and issues arising out of the assertion of identity of the major nationalities of the North-East adds a distinctiveness to the entire collection. As identity question/crisis is one of the issues being debated even today in the academic circle, this book provides immense information on the underlying problems faced by many of the tribal societies of N.E. India.

The edited volume *Sequences of Development in N.E. India* by J.B. Bhattacharjee (1989) is an outcome of the Seminar held at Shillong under the same theme in 1985. The volume contains papers on the study in the development process of the challenging region of N.E. India. The authors through those 25 research papers try their best to trace the different stages in development retrospectively, identify the constraints — political, social, cultural and environment and suggest measures to overcome these constraints as well as provide strategies how to work out to meet them. Though some of the papers discussed and highlighted the problems/sequences of development from the economic, social and cultural aspects, many other papers also analysed the sequences of development in the region from the political angle. Such papers are therefore of immense help to students of Political Science by way of looking into the issue from the point of view of the concerned discipline. The question of tradition, continuity and change as the sub-title suggests is brought into focus by a number of contributors. The issue of tradition — modernity dichotomy — either the presence or lack of it — also finds its place in some papers. How far traditional mooring can be made use of as a background or the hindrances provided by tradition in the process of development is another important aspect that appears in some papers. The volume contains a number of case studies by the scholars who are the authorities in their respective areas and their knowledge of the intricacies of the problems confronting the North-East. They have probed what has or has not happened by suggesting why something could or could not actually come through as well as the possible alternatives and the tasks ahead.

Political Development of the North-East (Vol. I), edited by B.C. Bhuyan (1989), is a collection of papers presented at the Seminar on the political development of N.E. India in November 1986, at Diphu. The book contains a good number of interesting papers on various problems and issues relating to political development in N.E. India. Broadly speaking, the various papers can be categorised into three groups — first, the problem of inter-State relations and boundary disputes in

N.E. India; second, the emergence and role of regional political parties in N.E. India; and third, the autonomy movements in N.E. India including that of the Autonomous District Councils. These papers are helpful in the sense that the authors had discussed many sensitive issues and problems facing N.E. India. The papers have therefore enriched our understanding of the political issues, problems and development of the North-East from time to time.

Tribal Identity and Tension in North-East India by B. Datta Ray (1989) discusses the much talk about issue, that is, tribal identity in N.E. India. Many problems, tensions and movements took place among the people of N.E. India due to identity crisis. This crisis has its own uniqueness due to the region's geographical location and historical background. Christianity and education have also emerged as strong factors of modernisation and have given the tribals a sense of identity. With the emergence of the educated elite among the tribal people, this group tried its best to take the lead in the ethnic assertion. The book besides an Introduction, has chapters like — Ethno Cultural Situation, Observation from Field Studies, An Overall Assessment of the Ethnic Situation and a Conclusion. The book adds more resource and reference materials on the problem/issue of Ethnic Identity in North-East India.

The book *Social & Political Institutions of the Hill People of N.E. India* (Eds.) Jayanta Sarkar & B. Datta Ray (1990) consists of papers presented in the Seminar held in 1977. Majority of the papers discussed about the social and political institutions of the 'hill people' of N.E. India and also highlighted the nature and extent of changes that have occurred after Independence, due to exposure to the federal, democratic polity of the country and its politics. About one-third of the papers included in this volume was contributed by scholars hailing from among the hill societies themselves and thus the book gives an insider's viewpoint. The book will be of great interest to students of Political Science who are interested in the study of traditional-socio-political institutions of the hill people of N.E. India.

The book *North-East India: A Profile* by M. Horam (1990) is a collection of articles written by the author over the past fifteen years or so on different aspects and issues concerning North-East India. These articles were published in different books, journals, magazines, etc. The author compiled them together in a book form (the present volume). These articles may be of good use to students and researchers who are interested in the problems faced by North-East India. Going through these articles, it may be said that they are relevant and create a lot of interest for students of Political Science. The author has actually discussed most of the sensitive political issues concerning North-East India. These articles therefore contribute to an understanding of the problems of the region in general and the tribal population in particular. The articles provide ready reference materials on political problems and issues of North-East India.

The volume on *Nationality, Ethnicity and Cultural Identity in North-East India*, edited by B. Pakem (1990) was the outcome of the Seminar proceedings held in Shillong by the NEICSSR in 1986. The proceedings have indicated as the title of the book suggests that these three pertinent issues—nationality, ethnicity and cultural identity have assumed a multidimensional importance in view of the urgent need for economic, social, cultural and political development of N.E. India. Regional economic development can be sustained on rational policy, forms and strategies for the achievemnt of the goal of overall development of nationalities consciousness of their distinct identities. The authors of the various papers discussed the issues of national formations in proper perspective and the questions of nationalities, ethnicity and cultural identities were examined and analysed in a scientific way. The book will be of great help to students of Political Science interested in those burning issues prevailing and facing N.E. India today. The different papers containing in the book therefore provide enough resource materials, as far as N.E. India is concerned.

I. Assam

Before 1963, there was only one State for the whole of North-East India, that is, the then composite or undivided Assam. In 1963, the State of Nagaland was created. Even after the creation of Nagaland, most of the literature on Assam discussed not only about the plain areas of Assam but the hills too. Against this background, it is therefore obvious that a good number of literature would be on the political, administrative and constitutional history of Assam. The literature on Assam which were published in the 1970s, dealt with Assam in particular and other areas in N.E. India in a general way. There are a good number of books during the period of review which specifically discussed and examined the problems of Assam. These books dealt mostly with revenue administration, administration of the hill areas under Assam, etc. One prominent issue discussed was on the reorganisation of Assam and the creation of six more States thereof. Also during the period under review, the most prominent issue discussed and critically examined is the movement led by the AASU in particular and the people of Assam in general on deletion, detection and deportation of foreign nationals from Assam. Some authors have also highlighted on the Assam Accord and the issues emanated from it. Insurgency in Assam and the role played by the ULFA has also been critically highlighted.

A Descriptive Account of Assam by William Robinson was originally published in 1841 and reprinted in 1975. In this book, the author has outlined the general account of the areas then known as Assam with a sketch of the local geography as well as a concise history of the tea plantation in the area. But what is of great importance is his description of the neighbouring tribes giving elaborately their history, manners and customs. But for students of Political Science, chapters on Political Geography, Civil and Social State, and the description of the Hill Tribes will be of great interest and help to understand the earlier socio-cultural and political development of the region which was then under the composite State of Assam.

The book *Assam Secretariat (1874–1974)* by B. Datta Ray (1978) traces the growth of the Assam Civil Secretariat during the period 1874–1974 and deals with some aspects of the Assam P.W.D. Secretariat. The method of approach used in the book is essentially historical, analytical and critical. The book contains eight chapters. The first two chapters deal with the historical growth and structure of the Assam Secretariat and

Departments. Third, Fourth and Fifth are concerned with personnel administration. The Sixth and Seventh chapters deal with the Rules of business and auxilliary services, and the final chapter contains conclusions arrived at different chapters.

Besides tracing the historical development of the Assam Secretariat, the author also tried to explain that the Secretariat was not made at any time by the wisdom of one man or few persons. The author suggested that the Secretariat should confine itself to policy formulation, consequent legislation, coordination of the activities of the various agencies and general policy direction. The study is based entirely on government records available in the Assam Secretariat Record office. The book will be of help to students of Political Science especially those interested in the field of Public Administration.

The author of the book *Public Service Commissions — A study*, Niru Hazarika (1979) traces the history of the establishment and presents necessary information that led to the evolution of the Public Service Commission in Assam. The book also deals with the organisation, the various functions of the Public Service Commission and its relationship with the Government and its other bodies. The opinions expressed by responsible persons in different services threw light to the condition that was prevailing in Assam for establishing a PSC in the area when Assam was only a Province. The author in trying to trace the evolution of PSCs went through the reports and opinions of various agencies like — the recommendation of the Simon Commission, India Committee (London), White Paper on Indian Constitutional Reforms, Joint Select Committee and the Government of India Act, 1935. The opinions given by the Governor of Assam at that time and other high government officials were also taken into account. The author has extensively made use of the original record and sources available, the regulations of other PSCs in the country, the reports and rules of various departments of Assam Government and other sources. The numerous suggestions put forward by the author in the concluding chapter are important and thought provoking. The book will be of great help to the civil servants in general and to students of Public and Personnel administration in particular.

Report on Assam by A.J. Moffat Mills (1980: Reprint) is a new edition of the *Report on the Province of Assam* (same author) (1853) and submitted to the Government of Bengal. The present volume deals with six districts of Assam — Goalpara, Guwahati, Lakhimpur, Nowgong, Sibsagar and Tezpur. There are separate reports on every district on a number of aspects. Besides a discussion of the mode of administration of each district, this report provides a general sketch of the system of administration of many departments and contains several suggestions to improve the fiscal, civil and criminal administration of the country, to extend the cultivation and to develop the resources of the Province of Assam.

Supported by a large number of tables and appendices which include correspondences among British officers, the present volume is an invaluable historical document on the erstwhile Province of Assam. The Report is an indispensable reference source to students and teachers of History and Political Science.

The book *Assam in the Days of the Company (1826–1858)* by H.K. Barpujari (1980) is a critical and comprehensive book on the political history of Assam during the rule of the East India Company (1826–1858). The book is based on original Assamese and English sources, both published and unpublished. Though historical in approach, the book contains an immense source of background materials for students of Political Science, especially those who are interested in administrative and political devlopments during those hectic days of the Company's rule. Also, the information provided in the book helps in building up good grounding base in understanding the administrative and political history of Assam before and after the changing of hands in administration from the Company to the British Crown.

Assam: A Crisis of Identity by Sanjayya (a pseudo name) (1980) is one among many such books which came out after a long drawn agitation in Assam led by the AASU and others against foreign nationals in Assam. The author based his writing on the basis of his tour of Assam and Tripura where he interviewed a cross-section of the population. The book begins with the glimpses of the past history of Assam; the creation of the new nation of Bangladesh, and its aftermath.

The author also analysed the situation that took place in Mangaldai, where the problem emanated. The other chapters of the book include like the intensification of the struggle, the talks between the AASU, other organisations and the Central Government, and the beginning of the crackdown. Two Appendices are also added to the chapters — one on the turmoil in the Nort-East and the other on the Constitution of India (Part II). On the whole, the book endeavours to describe and analyse the issues and factors that led to the movement in Assam and the response of the Government of India or the lack of it, which brought about a number of other knotty problems not only for Assam but the whole of N.E. India. The book does contribute to an understanding of the political situation in Assam during the 1970s and 1980s.

A small booklet *Eclipse in the East: An Analysis of the Present Agitation in Assam*, Assam Sahitya Sabha (1980) tried to analyse the movement in Assam against the foreign nationals. Like other books on the same problem, this one also dwelt to a certain extent on the factors that were responsibe for organising such a movement by the people of the State. The book described the magnitude of the problem due to the influx of foreign nationals to Assam, based on statistical data. The Assam Sahitya Sabha called this movement — 'a movement to defend the country' and expressed its fear in the pages of this book as a 'divide and rule' policy of the Government of India. On account of this influx of foreign nationals, Assam has been wronged in many ways — one of them is the sinister design of a sister State, that is, West Bengal. Like other books on the Assam movement, this one also adds some analysis to the whole state of affairs on Assam.

The small booklet of 33 pages only, entitled *North Eastern India: Problem and Its Solution*, by K.C. Chaudhuri (1980), endeavours to discuss and address mainly the political problems and issues concerning Assam, and offers some suggestions for their solutions. The author put the blame on the policy adopted by the Government of Assam and the Assamese leaders in 1960 towards the 'regional language' which had created much ill-feeling between Assamese and non-Assamese communities. This, the author opined, led to the break-up of the composite State of Assam into half a dozen separate political units. The after-effect of the Language Official Act of 1960 passed by the Assam Government then, gave way to a wide-spread movement of violent and disruptive activities all over N.E. India. The book throws some light on the burning issue of the 1960s and the aftermath it created. On the whole, the author tried to analyse an important milestone in the political history of Assam.

First published in 1906, *Provincial Gazetteer of Assam*, compiled by Authority (Reprinted 1983), is an authentic compendiumised study — from ancient times till early 20th century — of Assam's people and their history and culture, its geography, mineral resources, flora and fauna, religions, industry and trade, communication systems, public administration, albeit all kinds of information a researcher or general reader may need or may be interested in — at one place and sensibly arranged and put across. For students of Political Science, chapters on History of the Province, Government and Administrative divisions, Legislation and Justice, Finance, Land and Miscellaneous revenue, Local, Municipal and Public Works, as well as Police and Jail administration will be of great interest. These chapters provide basic information on these issues and therefore contribute a lot to our understanding of the political and administrative development of the province of Assam and other latter developments.

The book *A Century of Government & Politics in N.E. India*, Vol. I (Assam), 1874–1980, (1983) jointly authred by V.V. Rao and Niru Hazarika can be said to have followed immediately after the publication of a bigger volume on the general political developments of the whole of N.E. India. This volume is meant to cover the State of Assam's administration and politics during the earlier period and up to the time when the then composite State was reorganised into several political units. The authors dwelt at length on the administrative and political development that took place in Assam during the British rule and in the post-independence period. Assam in the pre-1963 period embraced all the other six political units of today. The authors have therefore discussed many political issues of those days which affected actually the whole of N.E. India. Many Acts, Rules, Regulations were passed by the British which affected both the plain and hill areas of N.E. India.

Different types of administration were also introduced by them. These and other important issues are discussed in the book. The post 1963 period in Assam politics is discussed and chapters on the NEC, politics of tension and inter-governmental relations are also included. An interesting topic on the role of women (both in the hills and plains of Assam) in State politics is an added dimension.

T.S. Murty in the book *Assam: The Difficult Years* (1983) tried to answer some basic questions faced by Assam and its people after the Assembly Elections of 1978. Assam during the period of writing of the book has been disturbed for more than three years. All the ministries formed during that period have been shortlived. President's rule has gone on longer than anywhere else. Hundreds of crores of rupees have been reported lost to the people because of the agitation — why all these happenings ? What are the reasons for these prolong agitations ? But the issue is not one concerning Assam alone. It affected other neighbouring States of Assam — like Meghalaya, Tripura, Nagaland, Mizoram, etc. The author tries to analyse many such thought provoking issues in this volume. The book makes an interesting study of the difficult years of political development and turmoil in Assam.

Assam Attitude to Federalism by Girin Phukon (1984) is an analysis of the Constituent Assembly debates which were in favour of a strong centre. This near unanimity view was widely held and no one deemed it necessary to question its validity. But this study has shown that during 1947–50, there was no unanimity on this question. The demands for greater regional autonomy began in the 1950s and continued even after when States/regions began to assert their personality a little more vigorously. Against this background, the author tries to analyse the views expressed by the Assamese elite both in the Constituent Assembly and the Legislative Assembly on the issue of granting more powers to the States within the scheme of Indian Federalism. Division of powers, distribution of financial powers and such miscellaneous issues —citizenship, emergency powers and Election Commission are also discussed by the author. The book contributes immensely to our understanding of the federal system of governance and Union-States relationship. The analysis tries to put things in proper perspectives which help in enriching the discipline of Political Science.

The author in this book *Assam: A Valley Divided*, Shekhar Gupta (1984) attempts to answer questions like — violence and ethnic frenzy in Assam, divisive politics played by both the Centre and the State, the question of linguistic, communal, land relations and socio-economic conditions of Assam. These questions had agitated the minds of the Assamese especially the elite of the society for many years during the Assam agitation period. The 1983 Assembly elections in Assam were put into proper perspective. The author also attempts to probe deep into the history of the Valley to answer the genesis of its alienation. In doing so, he assesses the role played by the tribals, the Bengalis, the Muslims and the countless "infiltrators" and "immigrants" in polarising the issue into an "indigenous-alien" one. Journalistic in approach, the book however provides interesting analysis of the situation in Assam.

Politics of Alienation in Assam by Bhawani Singh (1984) discusses the fundamental issues of dispute between Assamese and Bengalis on the focal point of State and national identity and the concept of political alienation amongst them. Divided into two parts — the first part deals with the land, people, conquest of Assam by the British and the constitutional development since 1947 upto 1983. The second part deals with the Assamese search for identity. A few suggestions have been made to solve the problem of internal migration to prevent further alienation of the Assamese people. Some of these suggestions are thought provoking and may be taken for further analysis by political scientists on the problem of alienation.

The book *Revenue Administration in Assam* by D.D. Mali (1985) covers the period from 1874 to 1920, and thus provides information about the Ahom period of administration not covered by S.K. Goswami's book mentioned earlier. Like the earlier book, this one may also interest students of Political Science to seek more information and detailed accounts of revenue administration in Assam.

The book *Development of Administration in Assam* by M.L. Bose (1985) traces the history of Assam as a province and its administration thereof. Secondly, it discusses the history of formation of the modern province of Assam — its administrative divisions and sub-divisions. The book also gives special reference to Land Revenue, Justice and Police administration between 1874–1920. The author endeavours through the chapters of the book to provide information and data relating to the administrative development in Assam under the period of study. The information contained in the book will be of great help to students of Political Science and this itself enriched the literature in certain areas of the discipline.

The book *Assam Issue: The Beginning — The End and the Beginning* by Vijay Kumar Dewan (1985) analyses the foreigner's issue in Assam as well as also the Assam Accord. It is one of those books which tries to analyse the situation that took place during those years of agitation in Assam on account of the foreigners' issue and bring out certain suggestions. As an author of various Law books, an attempt is also made here to look into the problem from its legal aspects based on the Constitution of India. Thus, constitutionl concepts like citizenship, nationality, domicile, residence, foreigner, etc. are brought in for discussion and analysed. The analysis of the Assam Accord is also given its due place in the book.

Assam: A Burning Question by Hirendra Nath Gohain (1985) is a collection of articles written earlier by the same author and some had been published in different newspapers of the country. These are the articles on the Assam Movement against foreign nationals and its background. The articles were written mostly in the later phase of the movement, though a few from an earlier period have also been included in this volume. The author tries to form an idea of the cross-currents in the movement and the forces giving rise to them in the first place. He also attempts a study of the development of the movement through different phases. The long introduction makes clear the links among the various articles as well as the standpoint from which they are written. A distinctive feature of the book is the approach to the basic issue through cultural history. The author sees in the complicated situation the travail of a small State caught up in the movement of gigantic forces of history, but makes no concession to negative chauvinism and secessionism. The book provides information and analysis on the Assam movement and its dimensions.

The book *Assam Muslims: Politics and Cohesion,* jointly authored by Bimal J. Dev and Dilip K. Lahiri (1985) represents an analysis of the dimensions and potentialities of Muslim Politics in Assam. The relevence of the issue has become all the more lively in view of the prolonged agitation on foreigners in Assam. Muslim politics in Assam has always been deeply entrenched in the arena of controversy largely because of the politization of apprehension by the caste Hindus. The authors have identified that in Assam the bond of religion is generally superseded by cultural identity and to that extent, Assamese Muslims are found to be culturally closer to Assamese Hindus rather than their Bengali compatriots. This penetrating analysis is an invaluable contribution in understanding the political consciousness and involvement of the Muslims of Assam who today find themselves at cross roads and among the vicissitude of political unheaval. They have also become the focus of the political turmoil in N.E. India. The book contains detailed analysis of the role of Muslim League in Assam politics and raises the question of immigration which is the great divide in Assam politics.

The book *A History of Revenue Administration in Assam* (A.D. *1228–1826*) by S.K. Goswami (1986) gives a detailed history of the revenue system of the Ahom rulers in Assam, from the beginning of the 13th Century to the end of the 18th Century. Though the author's approach is from the historical point of view, the book however provides indepth information of revenue administration in Assam during the Ahom rule. Students of Political Science who are interested in revenue administration may find the book to be of great help.

The book *Tai Ahom System of Government* by A.C. Sarma (1986) is an empirical work on the Ahom system of government with special reference to public personnel administration. The book provides information on the history of the Ahom kingdom (A.D. 1228–A.D. 1826) as well as the nature of government and the organisation of the administrative areas. Other chapters include such topics like Administration of Justice, Legislation, Revenue Administration, Foreign Relations etc. The author also makes a comparative study of the Ahom system with that of the modern. Students interested in political and administrative history of Assam during the Ahom period will find the book to be of interest.

Aspects of Revenue Administration in Assam (1826–1874) by Shrutidev Goswami (1987) is an attempt to present certain aspects of revenue administration of Assam between 1826, the year in which Assam passed under the control of the East India Company and 1874, when it was separated from Bengal and constituted into a Chief Commissioner's province. Based mainly on primary sources, both published and unpublished, the present work makes an objective study of revenue administration during 1826–1874. Although the focal point in this study is the admninistration of the various miscellaneous revenues, the author also takes care to highlight the main trends of the British economic policy in this trouble ridden frontier State during the formative period of British administration. Though historical in its approach, the book does provide basic information on the subject of revenue administration. Students of Political Science may make use of the historical background as provided by the author of the book for further future investigation. Students of Public Administration and also those interested in political history of Assam may find the book interesting.

This documentary study *An Account of Assam and her Administration (1603–1822 A.D.)* by H.K. Barpujari (1988) is an English version of an indigenous chronicle forwarded by David Scott, as an annexure to his elaborate report on 15 April, 1826 when the restoration of Ahom monarchy was under active consideration of the Governor-General in Council. The present book is a representation of the original translation of an Assamese Chronicle preserved at the National Archives of India. Political events apart, the book provides a glimpse into the system of administration and its woring during the period under review.

State Politics in India: A Study of Assam Legislative Assembly (1988) by Kunja Medhi is an analytical study of the State Politics in Assam with special reference to its Legislative Assembly during the period 1962–1972. Broadly speaking, the book is divided into two parts — the first one deals with the historical background and development of legislature in Assam. In this part, three general elections of 1962, 1967 and

1972, have been analysed; the role of Speaker, conduct of members, the Ruling Party's behaviour inside the House, House Committees, the Governor's role and the Role of Opposition are the chapters included. The second part includes an analysis of various social legislations including the problem of the reorganisation of Assam and its after-effect. The author has turned out a lot of data to prove the elitist nature of the Assam Assembly and the rural origin of the State managers did not facilitate rapport with the masses. Against this background, the book provides data and information to enrich Political Science literature in N.E. India.

Assam: From Agitation to Accord by H.N. Raiabadi (1988) is yet another account of the Assam agitation against the foreigners, the issues involved therein and the signing of the famous Assam Accord. When Shri Rajiv Gandhi (then Prime Minister) signed the Assam Accord, the nation believed the stormy days of the agitation were over. Unfortunately, this was not so. This only provided a new basis for the turmoil to continue. In this book, the author analyses the disastrous implications of the Accord on the State's minorities, especially the Muslims.

The first half of this investigation details the background to the agitation, makes an introduction to the Muslims predicament in Assam and discusses the implications of the Accord. The fourth chapter presents specific instances of the misuse of the provisions of the Accord. In the second half of the book, the actual documents concerning the Assam Accord are reproduced including the Accord itself and the various reactions to its implementation. These documents are important sources to understand the socio-political and constitutional backdrop of the agitation.

In recent years, a vibrant feature of North-East India has been the rise of ethnic consciousness leading to tribal movement and ethnic assertions and sometimes unrests. This vital problem needs a closer examination.

In the book *Dimensions of Tribal Movements in India — A study of Udayachal in Assam Valley* by Madan C. Paul (1989), the author tried to explain the various dimensions of tribal movements with special reference to 'Udayachal Movement' in Assam Valley. The attempt made here is to explore sociologically the genesis of plains' tribal movement of Assam Valley. The author's contention is that this movement has not come out from a vacuum. The contradictions introduced by the unequal socio-political forces in the tribal communal social system during the colonial era and the consolidation of the same in the post-independence period, challenged their existence. This in turn, forced the tribals to resort to various forms and types of movements. What is urgently needed, opined the author, is the radical transformation of the inequality, injustice and exploitation in one form or another. The book is of great help in understanding social movements in North-East India.

The book *Spotlight on Assam* by S.K. Das (1989) consists of the reprints of the articles written and published by the author in the *'Statesman'*, Calcutta, and the *'Economic and Political Weekly'*, Bombay. Each of the articles contained in the book has a separate background and specific approach. The general idea thrown by the author is first, to ventilate some of the issues of the vexed problem of foreign nationals in Assam and secondly to locate the real cause of Assam's deprivation. The author through these articles has tried to examine and analyse the long drawn agitation in Assam on foreigners issue.

The book *Revenue Administration in Assam* compiled and edited by D.K. Gangopadhyay (1990) traces the administration of Assam under the British and other administrative arrangements made thereof — including land revenue, revenue villages, towns administration, etc.; history of growth of Assam Secretariat since 1874 has also been discussed. A detailed picture of the evolution of administrative departments with special reference to Revenue Department, its present set-up and distribution of work has been given to facilitate the overall administrative milieu. This book updates the information (1990s) which are not available in other books written earlier. The book gives the readers detailed information on the revenue administration of Assam. The book does contribute and enrich the discipline of Political Science in certain areas of administrative and revenue administration.

The book *Roots of Ethnic Conflict: Nationality Question in North-East India* by Sajal Nag (1990) tries to probe into the question of nationality which has been one of the prominent problems faced by the present Indian political society. This book studies the nationality problem in Assam. It delves into the development of Assamese nationality beginning from the pre-colonial era, the advent of British capitalism and the consequent transformation. It analyses how the further development of Assamese nationality brought it into direct conflict with the more advanced and established Bengali nationality leading to perennial ethnic conflict culminating in the demand for eviction of Bengalis and transfer of Bengali Muslims dominated areas from Assam. The development of Assamese nationality and its conflict with the Bengalis became an interturned process. This process perceptively delineates the role played in the development of the nationality question by the various strata of Assamese society, viz., the peasant, the workers, the middle class, the intellectual, the elite and the politician. The work also attempts to unravel the complex interweaving of these elements in the fabric of Assamese nationality. The book provides a lot of information on the nationality question and ethnic conflict with special reference to Assam.

Manorama Sharma's book *Social and Economic Change in Assam: Middle Class Hegemony* (1990) mainly analyses the hegemony that the middle class has been able to establish over the Assamese society. This is done through the articulation of interests which are relevant to the large majority of the Assamese masses comprising largely the various sections of the peasantry. In the first chapter itself, the author attempts at conceptualising the term 'middle class' in general and its Assamese variant in particular. Sharma's analysis of the Assamese middle class is based on a study of social and economic changes in Assam in the period 1860–1910 — the period of the emergence and growth of the middle class in Assam as she calls it. The book may be of interest to students and researchers in the field of modern India's class formation, emergence of democratic politics and also the variants of peasant unrests in India and Assam in particular.

This book edited by P.S. Datta on *Ethnic Movements in Poly-Cultural Assam* (1990) contains besides the Introuction four other essays on ethnic movements in certain pockets of N.E.

India, mostly in Assam. Most of the hill areas of N.E. India with the exception of Karbi-Anglong do not find a place in the book. The book therefore concentrates within the limited jurisdiction of the State of Assam and basically analyses only the aspirations of different ethnic groups of the State, whose assertions have, by and large, been within the constitutional framework. There are four articles dealing with the Ahoms, Karbi-Dimasas, Koch-Rajbongshis and the Religious and Linguistic Minorities of Assam. The authors of these essays have collected relevant documents prepared and submitted from time to time to different authorities by various ethnic organisations and some of these documents have also been reproduced in the book. The articles and documents, taken together, provide an insight into the dynamics of the politico-cultural multiplex of Assam. The essays in the book provide interesting information on ethnic movements in certain parts of N.E. India with special mention of the minority communities of the State of Assam.

M. Kar's *Muslims in Assam Politics* (1990) makes an indepth study of Assam politics with special reference to Muslims who constitute about one third of the State's population. It gives a fully documented background to present day features of Assam politics on the basis of original records of the Government of Assam, Bengal and India as well as available private papers.

The author gives a systematic and chronological analysis of the coming of the Muslims and the politicisation of their migration, a basically socio-economic problem. He also traced the origin and development of the forces of contradictions and conflicts between the Assamese and the Bengalis. The factors leading to valley, linguistic, racial and communal animosities which ultimately resulted in complete community alienation despite centuries of their associations are important features of the work. The study also examines, analyses and assesses the Muslim's role in and contribution to Assam politics including the Freedom Movement and the demand for Assam's inclusion in Pakistan. Future portents of the State's politics have also been portrayed. The book adds to our understanding of yet another political dimension of minority politics in Assam.

II. Arunachal Pradesh

Arunachal Pradesh the once forbidden and formidable land is situated in the north-eastern most part of India attained its statehood on the 20th February, 1987. This mountainous State abounds with beauty of nature is sometimes described as a "hidden land". The then North-Eastern Frontier Agency (NEFA) which is now Arunachal Pradesh did not attract much attention of the scholars earlier. It was only after the Chinese invasion of India in 1962 that many people in the mainland of India came to know that this area is part and parcel of India and since then it has come to limelight and drawn the attention of a number of scholars. Prior to the British administration, there was practically no account available about the area. However, a more detailed account has been made available only after India's independence and the introduction of systematic administration thereof. The history of the administration of the area may be traced back to the Government of India's Notification of 1914. Prior to 1972, the area was popularly known as NEFA comprising of five districts. There has been few attempts to study and examine the political situation and administrative development of Arunachal Pradesh in the recent years. Some of these studies are reviewed here to know about the political development that took place in the State during the years under review.

Constitutional and Administrative Growth of the Arunachal Pradesh by P.N. Luthra (1971) is a book based on the Acts, Rules, Regulations, etc. passed from time to time relating to the administration of the then NEFA and the present State of Arunachal Pradesh. The book contains useful information on the administrative development and processes that had been introduced and implemented on NEFA (now Arunachal Pradesh). The various Acts, Rules and Regulations form a basic source of data and information on the administration of the State since 1914. Students of Political Science who are interested in constitutional history and political development will find this book to be of great help as a reference source. These sources can provide an immense source materials for further analysis of the political situation in Arunachal Pradesh.

J.N. Chowdhury's book *Arunachal Pradesh: A study in Profile* was first published in 1973 and the second reprint came out in 1992 (published by the Government of Arunachal Pradesh). As has been explained by the author, his purpose in writing the book was 'to present a profile of the traditional culture of the major tribal groups of Arunachal Pradesh'. In the process of momentous development activities stretching over more than three decades since India's independence, the tribal societies have inevitably undergone changes in almost all spheres of life, including the traditional mores of these societies. In the earlier volume, the author discussed about the international frontiers, the McMahon Line, genesis and evolution of administration in Arunachal Pradesh besides other topics. However, in order to give the readers some idea of the tremendous changes already brought about in the quality of life of the people, particulaly in political, constitutional and socio-economic spheres, the last chapter of the book has been revised and rewritten by the author. This chapter enhances the importance of the book for those curious readers wishing to have a quick insight into the then Union Territory, now the State of Arunachal Pradesh.

British Policy in the North-East Frontier Agency by Manilal Bose (1979) gives a detailed account of the social, economic and cultural life of the people inhabiting the frontier area of N.E. India which is now Arunachal Pradesh. The then NEFA has a long administrative history under the British. The main part of the study relates to the history and evolution of British relations with the tribes of the north-east frontier in the pre-independence times. The legal validity of the demarcation of the Inner Line and Outer Line is also considered in this volume and the British policy towards this stategic area is analysed. Besides other socio-cultural aspects, the book gives also an account from an administrative and political perspective. The three main chapters include — the Inner Line, the Outer Line and the McMahon Line; Administration of the N.E. Frontier and British Policy in the N.E. Frontier. The Appendices provide more information in the form of documents relating to administrative processes.

Arunachal Through the Ages by J.N. Chowdhury (1982) is a sequel to the author's earlier book *Arunachal Panorama*. The present volume is an attempt to trace the historical situations of the tribes of Arunachal from frontier tracts to Union Territory as the sub-title suggests. The author also discussed about the British advent, administrative involvement, the story of the MacMahon Line as well as the political and constitutional development leading towards the creation of the Union Territory of Arunachal Pradesh. Through this book vast information can be gathered on Arunachal Pradesh. The book has contributed greatly in understanding the different stages of politcal and administrative development of the State which till India's independence there was not much attempt to highlight its problems and issues.

Frontiers, a book by George Dunbar (reprinted in 1984) was first published in 1932. This account of the Indian frontiers, written by a former official of the Civil Service, deals essentially with the north-eastern frontiers of India, specially the present territory of Arunachal Pradesh. Despite its self-conscious search for the 'romantic' and the 'mysterious', the narrative provides, even now, many insights into the society and politics of the frontier people like the Abors, the Akas, the Mishmis, the Hill Miris, the Nishis as well as some Naga tribes. Above all, it helps to recapture the flavour of the past which, in the swift social and political changes that have come over the territory in the years since India's independence and even more so since its constitution as a separate Union Territory with limited self-government, can never be restored on the ground. The insights provided by the author in the book have a relevance even now to students of Political Science especially in the realm of administration.

The book *Administraive Development of Arunachal Pradesh* by Bijan Mohanta (1984) is a comprehensive account of the administrative development of Arunachal Pradesh beginning with the advent of the British in the N.E. Frontier region. The author also brought to light in the book the role of the civil servants in the development of administration in Arunachal Pradesh, tribal self-government in the then NEFA, Panchayat Raj administration as well as the birth of Arunachal Pradesh as a Union Territory and the administration thereof. The author traces the various stages of political and administrative development of Arunachal Pradesh as a Frontier Agency and as a Union Territory. The author in this book tried to highlight some of the earliest issues in the political development and administrative structure of NEFA and the changing role of administration in a few administrative set up of the Union Territory of Arunachal Pradesh. Such background information helps students of Political Science to have a background knowledge of what happened in a remote place like Arunachal Pradesh before it was upgraded into a State.

A.C. Talukdar's *Political Transition in the Grass-roots in Tribal India* (1987) is an attempt to investigate the nature of political transition at the grass-root level through the functioning of Panchayati Raj in Arunachal Pradesh. The book aims at inquiring into the impact of the working of the Panchayati Raj on the traditional political institutions; the socio-economic background of the Panchayat and traditional leaders; attitude of the people and the leaders towards the panchayats and above all, the extent to which the panchayats are instrumental to political change and development. The book includes such chapters on an Introductory note on Arunachal Pradesh; the traditional village council, Introduction of Panchayats in Arunachal Pradesh and its impact thereof and the changing trends both at the grassroot leadership and the people in general. With the recent introduction of the Constitutional amendment (73rd Amendment), the book provides an interesting background to the working of the Panchayats in Arunachal Pradesh. The book also opens up the issue of relationship between the traditional political institutions and that of the modern constitutional set up, thereby entering into a debate of tradition-modernity dichotomy. From this angle, the book forms an interesting study from Arunachal Pradesh which will be of great interest to students of Political Science. On the whole the book contributes something to enrich the discipline itself and becomes an indispensable source of reference.

The book *Emergence of Arunachal Pradesh as a State* by Chandrika Singh (1989), gives an exhaustive account of the history of the people of the State — their origin and the processes of political development leading to the emergence of Arunachal Pradesh as a State. It also presents the working of democratic processes in the State, the political and cultural behaviour, activities and response to the constitutional democratic system of India. The book not only provides information about the administrative set up during the British period and as a frontier area under a particular administrative arrangement (NEFA) but also brings out and analyses the political developments leading to the emergence of a full-fledged State.

Arunachal Pradesh: An Overview by Parul Ch. Dutta (1989) is a short handbook projecting the image of the fascinating land in the North-Eastern corner of India. This book though short, provides the basic information about Arunachal Pradesh — its people, geography, their history and administration of the State during the various stages of its development. The book will be of interest to those who want to have a bird's eye view of Arunachal Pradesh. Basic information about the State and its people is also given by the author.

III. Manipur

Manipur was earlier a princely State. After independence, it became one of the Union Territories and following the reorganisation of Assam in 1971, it was established as a full-fledged State. Thus Manipur has a long political and administrative history. Most of the books under review during 1970–1990, examined this long period of political, administrative and constitutional development of the State. Many Acts, Rules and Regulations were passed from time to time right from the British period of administration. Manipur also had its own kings who ruled over both the hills and plains. This is another area of investigation and concern for those scholars who are interested in the political development of the State. Another problem which attracts the attention of most of the scholars on Manipur after independence is insurgency. The mushroom growth of insurgent groups in the State gives rise to secessionist movement and this has created much badblood between the people of the State and the Central Government. Insurgency problem is of course still very much alive in the State. Along with this problem, a number of other serious problems have also raised their ugly heads in the State. Many scholars have therefore tried to examine the constitutional development, the problem of insurgency, smuggling of narcotics and the question and role of the neighbouring countries in the politics of Manipur. Other issues which appear prominently on Manipur politics are electoral politics, role and functions of political parties, formation of Governments and politics thereof in the State and the crisis of ethnicity and identity especially among the Meiteis and other tribal groups inhabiting Manipur.

R.P. Singh's *Electoral Politics in Manipur (A Spatio-Temporal Study)* (1981) analyses the political behaviour of the electorate in Manipur, a land of rich cultural heritage and equally fascinating politics. The author studied the electoral politics of the State in the light of her ecological setting during the Fifth General Elections held in 1972. It surveys the previous elections as they had a definite bearing on the 1972 elections. The author also peeps into the anatomy of the constituencies, analyses the party manifestoes, background of candidates, campaign processes, poll verdict, voting and its determinants in the spatial perspective.

The study which is rich in data and analytical in approach, helps in understanding the complexities of the electoral processes of Manipur. Inferentially, it also offers an insight into the various politico-integrational processes in a State, the socio-cultural asymmetries and pluralities of which have posed baffling problems. More specifically, the study brings out how the recruitment of a new strata into politics is causing the displacement of traditional elites. This makes the elite strata rather broad-based. But simultaneously, owing to its traditional character, the process also carries certain disintegrational implications with it. The book will surely enrich literature on electoral studies in N.E. India.

The book *Anal: A Tansborder Tribe of Manipur* by Gangmumei Kabui (1985) describes mostly the social and cultural activities of the Anals of Manipur. On political aspect, a small chapter appears where the author describes the village polity, constitution of a village and chiefship. The Anals are politically organised at the village level; chiefs and their councillors administer the village lands, maintain law, order and justice. The coming of democratic norms with India's independence has affected the Anal political system. This chapter will be of more interest to students of Political Science.

The book *In Search of Identity*, edited jointly by H. Kamkhenthang, S.P. Vaiphei, et al. (1986), is a serious attempt by the local scholars to find out and answer the question/ issue of identity of the Kuki-Chin groups of Manipur. Under the auspices of the Kuki-Chin Baptist Union, five local scholars contributed papers on the issue of 'identity' of the Kuki-Chin people. The contents besides the Introduction include 'Groping for Identity' 'Who we are/Who are we', 'Who are we' and 'Why should we be called Zoumi'. The problem/ issue of identity crisis is troubling the whole of N.E. India even today. The articles presented in the book also try to answer and make a searching attempt to answer the question of the identity of the Kuki-Chin people from the Christian perspective. Students of Political Science who are interested in searching information on the identity crisis with reference to the Kuki-Chin groups will find the book to be of great help. The experience of these people of Manipur may also be made as a reference point in trying to understand the issues of ethnic identity, ethnic assertion and movements in other parts of North-East India.

The Paite Customary Laws were compiled by G. Thangchinlian and T. Jamkhanthang (1986). The need for having the customary laws of the Paites in a written form has been felt for a long time. Whenever the need for application of customary laws arose, one has to run here and there asking the elderly persons as to how a particular case had been settled in the past. This practice is a cumbersome one and caused a lot of inconveniences to the present general public among the Paites. To meet the dire needs, the Paite National Council set up a two-man commission to compile the customary laws of the Paites. Thus, this book. This volume therefore provides basic information about the customary laws of the Paites. In the area of tribal studies, the book contributes an immense source of information. Student of Political Science interested in the customs, traditions and usages practised in the past will find the book an interesting one. Also in the area of traditional administration of justice this kind of books throw more light on the pristine institutions of the tribal communities and thus has its own weight in enriching our understanding of the socio-political history of the people of the area under study.

Manipur: Culture and Politics by Bimal J. Dev and Dilip K. Lahiri (1987) is a valuable contribution on the history, culture and politics of Manipur. The analytical framework of the book has unfolded the various dimensions of life, culture and politics in a most creditable manner and the authors have attempted to write an empirical treatise on Manipur. This book helps in trying to understand the cross-currents of the political life of the State. Secondly, the authors feel that insurgency in the State is a human problem definitely rooted in wounded pride of its people and hence a proper assessment of the emotion and sentiments of the people is necessary for initiating corrective measures to combat it. The book enriches the political analysis of the situation in such a difficult State like Manipur where besides politics, there is also a juxtaposition of many other factors.

The Naga Tribes of Manipur by T.C. Hodson (reprinted in 1989) was first published in 1911. The book describes about the Naga tribes living in the present State of Manipur. The author laid more stress on the social and religious practices of the people. The chapter which will be of interest and help to students of Political Science and the discipline is the one on Laws and Customs in which the author discussed about the Tribal organisations and institutions and their role in the traditional system of administration among the people.

The Meitheis by T.C. Hodson (reprinted in 1989) was first published in 1908. The book describes about the Meitheis of Manipur — their habitat, occupation, laws and customs and religious belief. The author laid more stress on the social, cultural and religious belief of the people. The chapter which will be of interest and help to students of Political Science and the discipline itself is the one on Laws and Customs of the Meitheis. In this chapter, an emphasis is made by the author on the political organisations, traditional institutions and chiefs that prevailed among the people. This chapter gives an analytical background on some of the traditional political institutions prevailing among the Meitheis in the past and the various activities and practices conducted by the institutions and those persons of the society who were responsible for running the administration.

IV. Meghalaya

As stated in the Introduction, the 1960s proved to be an event-ful years of political movements in N.E. India and more particularly in Khasi, Jaintia and Garo Hills districts of the present State of Meghalaya. Though the two Autonomous District Councils (ADCs) for the Khasi-Jaintia and Garo people started functioning since 1952, the leaders of these districts were not satisfied with the kind of 'autonomy' granted to the ADCs. It was actually, (Late) Capt. Williamson A. Sangma, the then Chief Executive Member (CEM), Garo Hills ADC, who convened the Conference of all the CEMs at Tura in 1954 to discuss about the Sixth Schedule to the Constitution of India. One of the resolutions passed during the Conference, was a demand for more autonomy to the ADCs in the hill districts of Assam as they did not enjoy 'real autonomy'. To cut short, the other resolution passed was a demand for a separate hill State. The hill State movement then became one of the serious and major starting points to analyse the political issues, problems and developments in Meghalaya in particular. The later decades saw an increasing number of literature attempting to analyse the political situation in Meghalaya at the beginning of the 1970s.

Most of the literature on Meghalaya dwelt at length on the issue of hill State movement, the formation of regional political parties, especially the APHLC and HSPDP, and their role in the formation of an autonomous State and later the full-fledged State of Meghalaya. Books written during the early 1970s described at length on the various plans, proposals and pattern of administration offered to the people of the State by the Government of India from time to time and their rejection one after the other by the leaders of the hill State movement in particular and the people in general, till the achievement of getting their own State as they demanded. During the period, a critical assessment of the Sixth Schedule and the working of the ADCs in Meghalaya also found a prominent place. When the State came into being, a number of questions were debated on the relevance of the ADCs in Meghalaya, their relationship with the State Government and other political aspects and developments form an interesting piece of literature. Formation of Governments by different political parties — both national and regional, has really enriched the literature on political studies as far as Meghalaya is concerned.

Kamleshwar Sinha's book, *Meghalaya: Triumph of the Tribal Genius* (1970) is one of the earliest attempts to analyse the historical political developments during the 1960s and 1970s leading to the formation of the State of Meghalaya. The book gives the background of the hill State movement and the various plans and proposals offered by the Government of India to the people of Meghalaya before the Autonomous State came into being and finally the full fledged State. Other chapters include like the Bardoloi Sub-Committee, the Sixth Schedule, the SRC's visit to Assam, the Autonomous State Plan, Meghalaya Act and NEC Bill. Besides the discussion on the people of Meghalaya, the author also brings into the picture the main tribes of N.E. India and discussed about the tribal genius. The text of the Sixth Schedule is provided in the book. Along with this, there are chapters on the APHLC, findings of the Bardoloi Sub-Committee and Pataskar Commission. Plans and Proposals like Nehru Plan, Scottish Pattern Plan, Pataskar Commission, the Federal Scheme and the Asoka Mehta Committee are also included in the book. The book is of great interest and forms an indispensable reference source for the study of Meghalaya politics since its inception as one of the States of the Indian Union.

The book by P.C. Kar on *British Annexation of Garo Hills* (1970) provides an outline account of the British annexation of Garo Hills and the pattern of administration introduced and enforced by the British authority. Besides the Introduction which gives an account of the social life of the Garos, the book contains three main chapters — Early Period of Annexation, Period of Expansion and Period of Consolidation. The Appendices given at the end of the Chapters provide interesting information on the British administration and its expansionist policy towards Garo Hills. The book forms another source of important information on the early phase of British administration in Garo Hills.

Hamlet Bareh's book on *Meghalaya* (1974) highlights the cultural heritage of the Khasis, Jaintias and Garos. The rich folklore, mythology, historical events, democratic institutions and other pristine institutions are also discussed by the author. A student of Political Science will find interesting historical accounts and Political developments leading to the formation of the Autonomous State and later the full-fledged State of Meghalaya helpful. Besides this, two other chapters on Provisional Government and Disrict Council's administration provide information on the political developments and processes during the hill State movement as well as the type of provisional government and administration during those two crucial years of an Autonomous State. Further political developments are discussed in the chapter on Meghalaya as a full-fledged State. The District Councils and their administration are also discussed especially on the power and functions of these Councils.

The book *Notes on Khasi Law* by Sir Keith Cantile which was originally published way back in 1934 and reprinted in 1974, has been recognised as one of the standard works on Khasi custom of inheritance, land tenure system and the traditional institution of Khasi Chiefs. The book highlights on many aspects of these customary and traditional institutions of the Khasi society. But even students of Political Science can immensely get the benefit from the book as it deals with very important aspects of socio-political life and institutions of the people. The book forms an indispensable reference source especially to those who are interested in knowing more about the issue of inheritance, social customs, land tenure system and the power and functions of the Khasi chiefs.

Principles of Khasi Law by A.S. Khongphai (1974) endeavours to describe and analyse the principles of Khasi law — inheritance, marriage and divorce, guardianship and adoption, gift and will, and maintenance. Though the author's approach is from the legal point of view, the book, however, will be of much help and interest to students of Political Science who are interested in the study of the traditions, customs, usages and practices among the Khasi and Jaintias in particular. These areas of social dimension cannot be overlooked by the students of the discipline while searching detail information on the tribal customary practices. The book also contributes to our understanding of the changing situation brought about by the new constitutional set up like the Autonomous District Council and its effects on those traditions, customs and practices of the people.

The book *The Khasi Canvas* by J.N. Chowdhury (1978) is divided into two parts. Part I as the sub-title suggests, deals with the cultural history, and Part II deals with political history of the Khasis. The later part of the book dwells at length with the earlier political history of the Khasi people right from the time when Khasi Hills' administration came under the British rule. The author also discussed about the political events before and after India's Independence including political developments leading to the formation of the State of Meghalaya. The author attempts to analyse the political situation and development in Meghalaya with the background of the British administration. The hill State movement which forms an important milestone in the political history of Meghalaya was also examined to provide an understanding of the minds of the people during those formative years of the struggle for their own State and the fulfilment of the same.

Electoral Politics in Meghalaya, edited by B. Datta Ray (1978) is a micro level study of the Sixth Lok Sabha elections from the two Parliamentary constituencies in Meghalaya. The book tries to state the main trends of politics of the State during inter-election years to serve as a backrop for understanding the electoral politics of the Sixth Lok Sabha elections. Manifestoes of the State and National political parties, politics of nomination and electoral alliances are parts of analysis of this study. Issues (political and non-political), strategies and styles of election campaigns, both at the State and local levels formed another area of discussion and analysis. The poll verdicts and their meaning for State politics in terms of causes, success and failures of various political parties in the field have also been analysed. Earlier Parliamentary election results have been reproduced in the Appendices. The results of the 1971 Meghalaya Legislative Assembly elections with a short analysis of voting pattern have also been shown as background statistics. The book is of great importance as a reference source on electoral studies.

A Collection of Writings about Khasi Hills and Khasis by Kynpham Singh (1979) details some of the author's attempt to inform the readers through his writings about Khasi Hills and the Khasi people. Some of the articles published in this book will be of interest and help to students of Political Science as these articles analysed certain important aspects of Khasi Hills like — administration of the *Syiem* of Khyrim, David Scott in Khasi Hills and the arrest of Tirot Sing, the *Syiem* of Nongkhlaw by the British. Though historical in presentation, these articles do contribute something to our understanding of the political situation in Khasi Hills, especially during the British period of administration.

Kollol Sen Gupta is his book *Without Roots* (Part I & II), (1979), describes the social tension between the tribals and non-tribals of Shillong during the 1970s. In the book, the author makes an endeavour to plead for settlement of Bengalees who had come to stay in Shillong after the partition of the Subcontinent. The author tries to weave the issues and problems faced by these displaced persons and advocates for an approach towards the amelioration of their plight. The book is therefore an attempt to place before the readers the continuous cry of the suffering minorities. On the whole, the book endeavours to look at one side of the problem — the problem of the linguistic minority group. The book is full of description on the social relations and tension in the capital city of Shillong.

This book *Local Government in Khasi Hills* by Umasaday Bhattacharjya (1980) attempts to analyse the institutions of local government at the grassroot level which have been one of the pillars of Indian administrative system. Particularly among the tribal people of N.E. India such traditional institutions which existed since time immemorial have played an important role. The practice of self-government among the Khasis is well-known; the people managed their socio-economic, political and cultural affairs through their traditional institutions like the office of the *Syiem,* etc. This book studies in historical perspective about this unique organised system of self-government among the Khasis with special reference to Syiemship. Other chapters include like — the Khasi Hills Autonomous District Council — its formation, working, powers and functions, elections to the Council, etc. The book also discusses about development of Shillong Municipality, elections, membership, functions, sources of revenue, grants-in-aid, audit and budget personnel administration including Government control over local government. The author draws his sources mainly from the official government records, acts, rules, regulations, gazettes and gazetteers of Municipality, District Council and some Syiemships; interview with the officials of these institutions was also made use. The main thrust of the book is on the Khasi Hills Autonomous District Council and the Shillong Municipality. The background materials and the analysis of the working of the traditional self-government among the Khasis will be of interest to students of Political Science interested in this area of study.

The book *The Origin and Early Hisory of the Khasi-Synteng People* by Namita Catherine Shadap Sen (1981) forms one of the most detailed studies hitherto written about the pre-history and history of the Khasi-Jaintia people of Meghalaya. The author attempts to record in logical form whatever reliable information she gathered about the past of the Khasi-Jaintia people. In gathering her material, she has utilised the evidence of archaeology, linguistics, written records and anthropology, as well as traditions and legends which have come to her notice from oral sources. Certain chapters of the book are more relevant to students of Political Science and the discipline. These chapters are — History of the Jaintia Kings (divided into three parts) as well as the History of the Hill Khasis along with the description of the Khasi chiefs, their role in the traditional system of administration, power and functions. Two chapters on Political and Social Institutions of the people under study also provide interesting accounts. In general, the book provides immense historical accounts of the past history and traditional socio-political institutions of the Khasi-Jaintia people.

The book *History and Culture of the Garos* by Milton S. Sangma (1981) is an account as its title suggests of the history and cultural patterns of the Garos. The book begins by giving a background description of the topography and the people living in Garo Hills. It then describes the traditional stories corroborated by ethnological and linguistic findings about their origin and migration from Tibet to the present abode, the Garo Hills. This is followed by tracing the political developments right from the ancient time to post-independence period. The book deals extensively with the varied policies adopted by the British resulting in the annexation of the hills into the British empire in 1866. It also discusses about the Inner Line Regulation, movements of the Garos against the British at the beginning of the 20th Century and the formation of political parties.

The powers and functions of the Village Council and village chiefs have also been analysed, followed by an account of other political institutions, traditional and the one introduced by the British. Traditional administration of Justice and the modern judicial system, both under the British and the Autonomous District Council form another important aspect of the book. Revenue administration from ancient time till present day is also discussed. On the whole, therefore, the book contributes immensely to our understanding of the social and political situation and history of the Garos. The book is an indispensable source of information on the Garos.

P.N. Dutta's work *Impact of the West on the Khasis and Jaintias* (1982) tries to trace the historical development that took place between 1765–1874. However, the author also gives a historical treatment regarding the people and their political institutions before they came into contact with the British. The author opines that the history of the Khasi-Jaintia Hills especially the early years of the contact with the British has some unique features. These hills (Khasi and Jaintia) were virtually the laboratory of British experiments in hill administration in N.E. India and the attempts to reclaim what was called, a primitive tribe to civilization. The model forged here was extended later on to other hill districts of Assam. Though this book treats the subject matter in historical approach, it contains a good deal of information both on the traditional political institutions of the people and the modern period of British administration. Students of Political Science will find the book to be of great interest in trying to analyse the British administration and its impact on the Khasis and Jaintias.

The book *Customary Law and Justice in the Tribal Areas of Meghalaya* by Kusum and P.M. Bakshi (1982) deals mainly with the laws and legal customs of the Khasis, Jaintias and Garos of Meghalaya. Though the book is written from the legal point of view, it does contribute to an understanding of the constitutional position and status of the tribal areas of Meghalaya. Moreover, the type of laws that prevailed among the tribal people of the State, the judicial administration, application and sets of instruments applicable to the people of the State, administration of justice at different levels of the Courts are discussed in details. The Constitution and the Tribal Areas is another important chapter appearing in the book. The question of inheritance of property, adoption, guardianship, marriage, divorce, maintenance, etc. are other important aspects of the book. In short, the book opens another kind of area of study and provides information to students of Political Science, especially from the point of view of the constitutional law and development. The book therefore provides guidelines to students of Political Science how to look into some of the pertinent issues among the tribal societies of North-East India from the legal and constitutional aspects.

The volume *Shillong 1971–1981* edited by B. Pakem (1984) is a collection of papers presented in the Symposium organised by the N.E. India Council for Social Science Research, Shillong, on December, 1981. The authors of the papers tried to assess and analyse what had happened in Shillong during the decade 1971–1981. Students of Political Science may get the benefit to enrich their knowledge about this cosmopolitan and an important administrative city of North-East India through some papers contributed by different authors on topics like —Shillong as an Administrative and Political Centre, Shillong Municipal Administration, Judiciary in Shillong, A Survey of Social Science Research Works conducted in Shillong, etc.

The book *A Century of Government and Politics in N.E. India, Vol. II, (Meghalaya: 1874–1983)* is the second volume of the series on a Century of Government and Politics in N.E. India jointly authored by V.V. Rao, B. Pakem and Niru Hazarika (1984). The present volume immediately followed the one on Assam (Vol. I). The volume as its sub-title suggests is on Meghalaya government and politics. The Reorganisation of Assam gave way to the creation of the State of Nagaland (1963) and the formation of an autonomous State of Meghalaya (1970) and a full-fledged State in 1972. The persistent demand for a separate hill State led to the formation of Meghalaya. The hill State movement is therefore discussed in detail by the authors. Government and politics under both the autonomous State and a full-fledged one finds its due place in the book. Formation of Government, Legislative Assembly, Administration of Justice, Local Administration, District Councils, Regional Political Parties and Union-State Relations are also included in the book. Even while discussing about government and politics in Meghalaya, the authors also included an analysis on the creation and working of the NEC. The book contains immense materials relating to the State of Meghalaya and its government and politics. The book is a great contribution to the literature on Political Science in N.E. India in general and Meghalaya in particular.

Hamlet Bareh's *The History and Culture of the Khasi People* (1985), (second revised and enlarged edition) was originally published in 1967. This book is considered the first of its kind on the subject and it is often quoted by scholars interested on the history and culture of the Khasi People. The book contains a detailed treatment on many basic subjects of ethnography, culture, politics and history. It provides exhaustive information on the associated topics, based on available sources of information. Though the book's title is on history and culture of the Khasi people, its contents include valuable information on the traditional polity/polity formation among the Khasi-Jaintia people. Besides the discussion on the traditional socio-political institutions, an exhaustive section relating to British relationship and administration and the impact/effect of the same on the traditional institutions and the society at large found due place in the book. In the second edition, the author has sought to enrich it by providing material for the reconstruction of the chapters and adding new ones, covering the period up to the formation of the State of Meghalaya. Though historical in its approach, students of Political Science may find the book very useful because of its rich resource materials. The book therefore contributes enormously to our understanding of the tribal politcal institutions with special reference to Khasi-Jaintia Hills and the political development that emerged after independence leading to the creation of a separate State of Meghalaya.

Tribal Institutions of Meghalaya edited by S.K. Chattopadhyay (1985), is a valuable collection of articles on the traditional socio-political institutions of Meghalaya. The book is divided into three parts. Part I deals with the indigenous institutions of the Khasis and the Jaintias, Part II deals with the indigenous institutions of the Garos, and Part III deals with the indigenous institutions of the State (Meghalaya) as a whole. The indigenous political institutions discussed in this book by various writers include that of the *Syiem*, the *Doloi* and *Nokma* among the Khasis, Jaintias and Garos respectively. The papers provide valuable background materials and information on these institutions which are in existence till date among the people of the State. Students of Political Science interested in acquiring knowledge about the indigenous institutions of the Khasis, Jaintias and Garos will find the book very helpful.

Bureaucracy and Development in Meghalaya by Debasish Bhattacharjee (1986), is the study as the title suggests on bureaucracy and development in Meghalaya with particular reference to the higher echelon of bureaucracy in the State. Though the author tried to trace the historical background of bureaucracy as such at the all India level, the scope of the book is however limited and restricted to higher bureaucracy in the State. The reason given being that it is this level of bureaucracy which is a managerial group and therefore more likely to have a direct bearing on political, economic and other kinds of development. The book emphasises the interaction pattern of bureaucracy with its environment as well as some of its behavioural feature in order to highlight the problems that the bureaucracy faces in the performances of its role as a major instrument of development in Meghalaya.

The book *Between Tradition and Change: A Perspective of Meghalaya* by Soumen Sen (1988), is a collection of occasional papers written at various times for Seminars, Conferences and Journals is a study of the sequences of development in Meghalaya. The author analyses the implications of change through a process of modernisation and development in a society where the people's lives are interwoven into their traditional systems. It is a study of the sequences of development, of tradition, continuity and change. Though the book is heavily loaded with essays on social and cultural change, it does contribute an analysis on emergence of middle class, politics of regionalism and political attitude of the people of Meghalaya. The analysis provided by the author will help the readers in understanding the issue of tradition and the changes that have taken place among the people of Meghalaya.

An attempt has been made in this book, *The Jaintias (Socio-Political Institutions of Jaintia Hills)* by S.K. Chattopadhyay (1988) to give an account of the Jaintia social institutions, ethnological affinities, religion, economy and the people's role in the entire gamut of their own society. The evolution of the political institutions and an analysis of the same is done by the author. Students of Political Science may find the two chapters of the book on Political Structure and Jaintias' conception of Republic and Democracy, interesting. The author has given his own viewpoints on these two issues which may be still debatable. On the whole, the book does provide certain data and informaion on the Jaintias' political institutions.

British Administration in Meghalaya: Policy and Pattern (1989) by D.R. Syiemlieh is a pioneering work. As the title suggests, it has two important facets of British administration in Meghalaya — their policy and pattern. The book covers the whole of Meghalaya in which its major inhabitants, the Khasis, the Jaintias, and Garos and their relations with the British are discussed by the author. The book examines the administrative milieu before the impact of the Raj and how and why the colonial power imposed their rule over these hills. The non-regulation system which was first applied in the hills became the hallmark of British administration in N.E. India. The book makes a detailed study of indirect administration through the traditional chiefs and the effects the new administration had on the socio-economic and political ethos of the people. Other sections analyse the administration of the twenty five Khasi states and the nature of control over these *Himas;* colonisation plans, the Crown Colony plan that never took shape; the revenue policy; resistance movements and concludes with an account of the legacy the British administration left behind for the Indian Government.

The book is a history of nearly two hundred years' interaction with the Britsh. It has an exhaustive documentation of recorded materials from various libraries in and outside India. Though historical in approach, the book contains rich source materials for students of Political Science.

The Editors, S.K. Chattopadhyaya and M.S. Sangma in the book *The Garo Customary Laws* (1989) bring out an interesting collection of articles on the Garo Customary Laws. Such documentation of the traditional customs, practices and usages that existed and practised by the tribal people in the past should be welcome and encouraged, otherwise these pristine institutions and fine traditions may be lost eternally due to the impacts and effects of modern constitutional institutions or modernity itself. Though majority of the papers deal with the socio-cultural, legal and religious aspects of customary laws among the Garos, the articles on administration of justice, chiefship (*Nokma*) and land disputes will be of great help to students of Political Science. Such articles, therefore, contribute certain interesting features which students of the discipline cannot overlook. On the whole, the book forms an important reference source on the Garos with special reference to their customary laws.

Meghalaya: Yesterday and Today by P.R. Kyndiah (1990) has much to present a package of information and knowledge to perceptive persons who would like to know more about the beautiful surroundings, the history and culture of Meghalaya. But for students of Political Science, two short essays — Emergence of Meghalaya, and Shillong: A Little England, may be of interest as they provide a short historical background to the hill State movement leading to the formation of the State of Meghalaya and the importance of its State capital — Shillong.

The book *The Khasis Under British Rule (1824–1947)* by Helen Giri (1990) is basically an attempt to trace the political and constitutional development that took place in Khasi Hills during the British rule. However, the author did not limit the contents of the book only to the British rule and administration. Besides this, the author tried to analyse and examine the Khasi way of life, traditional polity, laws of succession, the social and political system of the Khasis and the changes which have crept in. The materials used are archival documents, published and unpublished materials, discussions, interviews, etc. The author also tried to give a practical study of Khasi thought through its varied manifestations, social and political. The book will be of great help and interest for further understanding not only of the British impact of administration on the Khasi people but on their traditional political institutions, processes of political development and the changes therein. The Appendices provide an additional source of information. The book forms another source of political study on the Khasis in particular.

V. Mizoram

The then Lushai Hills (now Mizoram) was one of the districts of the then composite State of Assam for a long time after India's independence. Traditionally, the Mizos were under the administration of their chiefs and after the British annexation of the area, it was administered by them. The British Superintendent appointed to look after the administration of the area played an important role till 1947. Broadly speaking, the literature on Mizoram could be classed into two important periods — traditional and British period of administration and post-independence period. Some books described about the traditional leadership under the chiefs, their power, functions and role in the traditional system of administration. Besides this, many authors also examined and analysed the effects/ impacts of British administration especially the Superintendent, and the impact thereof on the Mizos, forms another interesting area of study and investigation. The literature on this aspect of the political history of Mizoram has really enriched the understanding of the political and administrative development in Mizoram. The post-independence period has its own unique contribution where scholars have described and examined the political situation in Mizoram during this period up to the present day. One of the most prominent issues discussed during this period was the insurgency problem in Mizorm, the role of the MNF in particular, the signing of the Mizoram Accord, formation of regional political parties, the formation of the Union Territory and later the full-fledged

State of Mizoram. In between that, the role of the Autonomous District Council and Regional Council and their relationship in the subsequent years with the State Government has also been highlighted prominently.

The Land Where the Bamboo Flowers by J.D. Baveja (1970), is one of the earliest attempts to understand the history of the Mizo people, their traditional culture and religion as well as their economy. The book also gives the author's view on the traditional socio-political institutions of the Mizos like the chief and his Council. Besides this, the modern administrative set up and political life of the people since the British days of administration till 1966 which was the turbulent period in Mizoram's history is also analysed by the author. Besides discussing the general traditional culture of the Mizos, the author also gives a detail treatment of the socio-cultural traditional institution like the *Zawlbuk*, which will be of immense interest to students of Political Science.

N. Chatterji in the small booklet on *Zawlbuk as a Social Institution in the Mizo Society* (1975), endeavours to trace the processes of evolution, working and functions, administration and the overall role and impact of this pristine social institution, the *Zawlbuk*, among the Mizos. This traditional social institution of Bachelors' dormitory played a very important role in shaping the youth of the society into responsible members. The system of Bachelors' dormitory among the Mizos produced excellent results in instilling into the minds of the young people from an early age, a sense of responsibility, discipline, a spirit of give and take and the service to persons elder than oneself. Such institution which prevailed in the earlier period of the history of the Mizos became a centre of social, religious and cultural activities. N. Chatterji has analysed these various aspects of the Mizo society through the institution of the *Zawlbuk* in this book. This kind of book produced interesting result and provided a lot of information. Students of Political Science interested in the studies of the traditional institutions will find it an indispensable source and guidance for future research on similar themes.

A Monograph on Lushai Customs and Ceremonies by N.E. Parry (Reprinted 1976) was first published way back in 1928 and the present volume is a reprinted version of the same.

This monoraph attempts to record the customs by which Lushais (Mizos) are governed in their daily lives and according to which cases are decided by the chiefs and the courts. This volume was written by the author when he came into contact with the Mizos with the hope that it will be of use to officers and chiefs engaged in the administration of justice in that district. Thus this compilation of the customs and ceremonies. The book therefore enriches our understanding of the customs of the Mizos. Students of Political Science interested in searchng deeper knowledge of the role, power and functions of the traditional chiefs among the Mizos will find the book to be of immense help. This book will be of great help in another area of study, that is, the traditional system of administration of justice among the tribal community — the Mizos.

Lal Biak Thanga's book, *The Mizos: A Study in Racial Personality* (1978), is one of the much sought-after books on the Mizos. The book gives the early history of the Mizos, their customs and religion, folklore, folktales, and goes on to discuss the advent of the British in Mizo Hills and the situation in Mizoram after India's independence. In the chapter on the early history of the people, discussion on traditional chief and institutions of the Mizos will be of interest to students of Political Science. Two other chapters — one on the British advent and relationship with the Mizos and the other on what happened to the Mizo Hills district after India's independence are also interesting as the author discussed the administrative and constitutional position of the Mizos during that period of time. The author analysed these political and administrative developments in great details. On the whole, this book contributes a lot to our understanding of the political and administrative situation in Mizoram in greater detail.

Robert Reid's *The Lushai Hills* was originally published way back in 1942 and the present volume was reprinted in 1978. The book gives a great detail of the Lushai (Mizo) Hills administration under the British and the long relationship between the two during the period it was held by the British authorities. The book describes the most important British expeditions between 1888–1890 of the then Lushai Hills and the major outcome of these incidents. The other four chapters analysed in detail about the British penetration, annexation and total involvement in the administration of the area. The other chapter discussed the Constitution Act of 1935 and how this Act worked regarding the Lushai Hills as one of the Excluded Areas. In terms of administrative and political development of Lushai Hills, the author has given an extensive discussion and analysis which enriched our understanding of the political situation during the period covered by the book. It is therefore an immense source of information as it provides enough background materials for the same.

The book *The Lushai Expedition (1871–1872)* by R.G. Woodthorpe was first published in the U.K. in 1873. The present volume (1980) is the reprint of the same. The British subjugation of Lushai Hills (now Mizoram) was an outcome of a series of expeditions. The author presents in this book a narrative of the earliest major expeditions to avenge the raids committed by the Lushais (Mizos). In order to ensure security of the frontier and to enable the British tea planters to carry on their operation in safety, the British policy towards the offending tribes was one of conciliation rather than retaliation. Departure, however, had to be made as the author has shown, when vital interests were at stake. The author has provided a mine of information as to the custom, usages and institutions of the Lushais (Mizos) particularly their mode of warfare, both offensive and defensive, tactics an strategies, stockades and fortifications. The book contains sidelights on the fortunes of the leading Mizo chiefs, their relations with one another and the rulers of the neighbouring native States like Manipur and Tripura. The book will be of considerable interest to researchers and students of Political Science as it contains a lot of information on the earlier British policy towards the Mizos and their chiefs in particular.

Nirmal Nibedon's *Mizoram: The Dagger Brigade* (1980) is the explosive story of the MNF struggle that persisted in the dense jungle of Mizoram. The author claims to have been able to penetrate the MNF and came upon a mine of information that had never been made public. The book is also based as per the author's claim on the recorded conversations with top Mizo leaders who either participated in the movement or were holding important positions during the height of the insurrections. The book therefore provides to the readers another important piece of information about the long struggle fought by the MNF for their people's freedom. The book contains chapters like Operation Jerikho, Operation Security, The Arakan Factor, besides others. The book adds to the understanding of the then turbulent situation in Mizoram during the heydays of the underground movement led by the MNF.

The book *Mizoram: Dynamics of Change* (1982) by Animesh Ray is often quoted by students and teachers as an important source on Mizoram. It contains a lot of information about the administrative history and development process in Mizoram up to its formation as a Union Territory under the Indian Union. The book depicts in historical retrospect the complexities faced by fascinating people, the Mizos, in a troubled situation of insurgency. The political, administrative, social and economic development of the people and the territory is the backdrop for the study of insurgency and counter-insurgency administration with overtones of social welfare and development administration. Chapters like — Consolidation of Administration, Role of the Church, Administration of Justice, District Council, Political Development, Insurgency, Situational Data (1973–82), Policies and Goals of Administration, could be found in the book which form many and diverse sources of information on Mizoram.

The Mizo Dilemma by Amit Kumar Nag (1984) discusses the problems posed by insurgency in Mizoram. The author is of the opinion that it is not only the problem of insurgency which is the dilemma of the Mizos but it involves a much deeper issue, that is, the rising ethnic aspirations of the people within the framework of national unity. The volume presents a modest attempt to place before the discerning readers the dynamics of change in the Mizo society against the background of genuine apprehensions and reasonable aspirations. Though the book is written from the journalistic point of view, it does provide certain information regarding politics and political development in Mizoram. The Appendices also form important sources of information for further understanding of the deeper aspirations of the Mizos in general and the MNF in particular during the heydays of the latter movement.

John Vanlal Hluna's *Church and Political Upheaval in Mizoram* (1985) is a study of the impact of Christianity on the political development in Mizoram. It traces the history of Christianity in Mizoram and examines its contributions in educational development and growth of public consciousness in the Mizo society, the identification of the linkage between the progress of Christianity and the politicisation of the community being the most significant contribution of the book. Though the book discussed in detail about the history of the Church in Mizoram, it did almost the same with its political history. There are four significant chapters on political development like — the working of the District Council, the revolt of 1966, role of the Church in Mizoram politics and Mizoram as a Union Territory and its administration thereof. The long documents reproduced in the Appendices contain huge information on the contemporary political history of Mizoram and these therefore will be of great help for further research on the subject.

Leadership Among the Mizos: An Emerging Dimension by P.K. Bandyopadhyay (1985) studies the Mizo people, their land and culture, as well as the influnce of various factors on the rural leadership structure and characteristics. Though the author's approach is socio-anthropological, the materials, sources of informaion and content, and data generated by him may be of great help even to the discipline of Political Science. The book provides information on the study of village/traditional leadership and the formal structure of authority at the grassroot level. The author based his data on case studies of four villages in Mizoram; therefore this book forms an important source for village studies with special reference to leadership pattern. Students of Political Science who are interested in village studies and trying to find out the leadership pattern of traditional institutions at the grassroot level will therefore find in this book certain profitable guidelines.

R.N. Prasad's book *Government and Politics in Mizoram (1947–1986)*, (1987), highlights the ethnological, cultural background and administrative set up of the Mizos, the growth of early politics resulting in the formation of the District Council for the Mizos and the Regional Councils for the Pawis, Lakhers and Chakmas of Mizoram to manage the local affairs by themselves. The book is one of the first efforts to study the politics of the people in the southern part of Mizoram. It further studies the MNF, violence, secessionism and counter insurgency measures. Political Parties/groups, their impact on socio-economic development, electoral politics and voting behaviour are also analysed by the author. The constitutional development and politics resulting in the formation of the Union Territory and later the full-fledged State for Mizoram has also been discussed. The study is largely based on interview and field work which have also been supplemented by primary and secondary sources of information. The book is an indispensable reference source to students of Political Science on the political and administrative development in Mizoram between 1947 to 1986.

A Century of Government and Politics in N.E. India (Vol. III) (Mizoram) (1987), jointly authored by V.V. Rao, H. Thansanga and Niru Hazarika, is the third volume of the main theme "A Century of Government and Politics in N.E. India". This volume details the administrative and political development of Mizoram. The volume is based as claimed by the authors on original sources available in the Assam Records Office, New Delhi, and the Deputy Commissioner's Office, Aizawl. The book begins with a profile of Mizoram and the constitutional development since 1947. The Mizo system of chiefship is one of the chapters. The other chapters deal with the Head of the State, the Legislative Assembly, Political Parties, District Councils, Administration of Justice, and Insurgency. The chapter on Insurgency gives a detail analysis how it started and the measures taken by the Government of India to curb it and restore normalcy. The book contains a lot of information on Mizo politics and political development which enriches as a source of literature on the discipline of Political Science with special reference to North-East India.

Mizoram Encyclopaedia (in three volumes) by Suhas Chatterjee (1990) gives interesting and valuable information about the Mizos and Mizoram. These volumes have been prepared quite thoroughly by the author to supply all available data and information about the Mizos and Mizoram put together in a book form. The volumes contain different topics on various aspects and also general information. These volumes may therefore be made use by students and teachers depending on what kind of information they would like to know about the Mizos and Mizoram. One may find in these three volumes the necessary references one may need. Sources and references have been cited and this forms ready references. Newspaper reports (both local and national) besides proceedings of research organisations and journals published from time to time have been used extensively. These volumes on Mizoram are therefore of great help as reference sources. Students of Political Science can also make use of the same as sources of data and information.

VI. Nagaland

Literature on political studies on Nagaland under the period of review is generally speaking based almost on the same problem and issues. Some literature on the political situation in Nagaland are to say the least, repetitive in nature. Most of the books stressed on the same issues. Beginning with the traditional society, the role of traditional institutions and chiefs among the different Naga tribes, most of the books went on to discuss the dominant issue of insurgency and secessionist movement led by A.Z. Phizo and his colleagues and the formation of the Federal Government by this group in Nagaland. The next area of investigation and analysis centred round the creation of the State of Nagaland in 1963, the formation and role of political parties, the ethnic and identity crisis among the Nagas, the signing of the Shillong Accord in 1975 and other agreements before that. Some authors have dwelt at length about these agreements, their interpretations, on one side by the underground Nagas and on the other by the Government of India and the problems attached to such agreements or their after effects. Electoral politics, the formation of different governments at the State level — both by the national and regional political parties form an interesting piece of political analysis of the situation in Nagaland during the period under review.

The book *Gazetteer of India: Nagaland (Kohima District)* edited by H. Bareh (1970) deals with the tribes of southern Nagaland, covering multifarious subject matters. Issues like general and revenue administration, Law, Order and Justice and Local Self-Government are also dealt with in this volume, which will be of interest to students of Political Science. The general information on administration including local self-government of this particular district in the State of Nagaland provides an insight into the state of affairs that took place during the time it was written.

The Rising Nagas (A Historical and Political Study) by Asoso Yonuo (1974) is an elaborate account of the Nagas for several centuries. It tries to update the information about them to the present day situation. Through the many pages of this book, one comes across various elements in the history of the people. The different stages of political processes and development, the socio-cultural activities of the people are to be found in the book. The author also discussed the earlier contacts and relations between the Nagas and their neighbours. An important space is also given in the book on the Naga-British relations and the administration introduced by the latter on the Nagas. When India got its independence, it has many problems to face with the Naga situation. Secession took place, insurgent movement took a deep root among the Nagas — these are important historical and political developments that shook Nagaland in the 1960s and even today. Nagaland was created as the sixteenth State of the Indian Union in December 1963. Even then things did not improve. Peace missions were formed; negotiations took place several times, agreements were also signed but all these did not help much in the long run. These and other important aspects of Naga life and politics are discussed by the author in the book. The book contributes a lot to Political Science literature as far as Nagaland is concerned.

The book *Nagaland: From a District to a State* by P.N. Luthra (1974), endeavours to trace briefly the events which led to the creation of Nagaland as the 16th State of the Indian Union. Shri Luthra has fully utilised his knowledge and first hand experience as an eminent administrator of the tribal regions of N.E. India to make a study in the political, administration and constitutional spheres of the State of Nagaland. Though the analysis part of the book is somewhat brief, the Appendices relating to Rules, Regulations, Acts, etc., passed from time to time concerning North-East in general and Nagaland in particular will be of immense interest and concern to the administrators and students of Political Science. Shri Luthra through those Appendices has made the relevant Rules, Regulations, Acts, etc. available to readers and the students of Political Science may therefore make use of them for further analysis.

The book *Naga Polity* by M. Horam (1975) makes a contribution towards the knowledge and understanding of early Naga political institutions which in many respects have not changed much even today. In order to study the Naga polity, one has to begin with the study of the family, village and the customary laws. These factors are very closely associated with the Naga polity. M. Horam did that in this book. The book gives an extensive study of the Naga polity especially at the grassroot level and the contribution made by such social institutions like the *Morung* and the village chief. These grassroot traditional insttutions play a very important role in understanding the polity of a tribal group. The book will be of great interest and help to those students of Political Science who are in search of knowledge about the traditional institutions and polity among the Nagas in particular and the N.E. tribals in general.

Conflict in Nagaland (A study of Insurgency and Counter-Insurgency) by V.K. Anand (1980) is one of the accounts among others which tries to critically analyse the conflict in Nagaland within the conceptual framework of insurgency and counter-insurgency. First, the book discusses the concepts with reference to insurgencies in other parts of the post-second World War. This provides an international context for the study of the problem in Nagaland. Beginning with the Nagaland scenario in 1946, the author traces the growth and ramification of the conflict through the next two decades to the gradual evolution of a political settlement in the seventies. The narration recreates the exciting events in a gripping style. The book, however, cautions against too much of optimism about peace in Nagaland. The peace it suggests may yet be elusive. Finally, the postscript indicates a connection between the Nagaland insurgency of yesterday and the mounting strife in the North-Eastern region today. The book is not merely a piece of military history. It is also a mine of information about the social and cultural life of the Nagas.

The book *Political Evolution of Nagaland* by Chandrika Singh (1981) was the result of the Ph.D. thesis, Magadh University. Though the author claims it to be an authentic book on the Naga polity, it does not however differ much from many other books written with the same intention. The book contains such chapters like — early history of the Nagas, the birth of Nagaland, Peace Mission, Shillong Accord, the working of the Democratic System and the changing face of Nagaland. Though repetitive in nature when taken into consideration of the other books written on almost the same problem, the book does help in understanding of the politics and political development in Nagaland.

B.B. Ghosh's *History of Nagaland* (1982) is a comprehensive work on the strategic eastern frontier State of Nagaland which was created in 1963. The author takes note of the physiography, flora, fauna, climate, population, religion, etc. of the State. Of course, the main emphasis of the book is on the history of the State from ancient to modern times. The author has tapped all available sources — archaeological, foreign travellers' accounts, records in the archives and other published and unpublished contemporary sources. Besides an exhaustive history of the State, the author also takes note of some of the distinctive features of the civilization of this remote and ancient land including social, cultural and economic aspects. On the whole, the book provides immense information on the political development and history of Nagaland.

Nagas Struggle Against the British Rule under Jadonang and Rani Gaidinliu (1925–1947) by Asoso Yonou (1982) gives a complete picture about what is popularly known as Zeliangrong movement led by Jadonang and Gaidinliu for the Nagas in late 1920s and early 1930s. This movement is one of the stimulating periods in the history of the Nagas for their freedom. The book describes in detail about the essentials of Naga animism, emergence of Jadonang and his execution, the taking over of leadership by Rani Gaidinliu, her subsequent capture, frantic efforts of Jawaharlal Nehru to release her from imprisonment and her role in the midst of problems like Phizo's uprising for Naga independence, and others of North-

East India. The book also details what may be loosely termed as 'Naga nationalism' in its nascent period. The book therefore contributes to our understanding of a movement among the Nagas in the early period of the history of the people of the State and the after-effect of the same in the subsequent years on Naga politics.

Hokishe Sema's book on *Emergence of Nagaland (Socio-Economic and Political Transformation and the Future)*, 1986, is yet another book on the Nagas. It gives an account of the origin, chivalrous disposition, social customs and the Nagas faith rooted in animism. Among such people like the Nagas, the ambitious British and the ambivalent missionaries made their inroads during the early nineteenth century. In the skirmishes that followed, the Nagas could not withstand the sweeping tide of the British imperialism and had to embrace Christianity. The rising Nagas and the slogan of an independent Nagaland under Phizo's leadership brought immense sufferings to the common Nagas' agony. The author tries to analyse these most pertinent questions and issues of his own people. In this book, Mr. Sema also narrates the inside story of the underground movement, reveals the concern of Pt. Nehru and Indira Gandhi for the peace and progress of Nagaland. The book has also such other chapters like Nagaland-Assam boundary issue, the Naga Sub-Nationalism and Looking Ahead, in which, the author tries to analyse the political aspirations of the Nagas.

Naga Insurgency (The Last 30 years) by M. Horam (1988). Many books have been written on the Nagas by non-Nagas especially those British administrative and army officers. Later many Indian scholars also ventured to write on the Nagas. This book is a major research work by a Naga himself and therefore presents to the readers an insider's view, that too, on a very touchy problem — Insurgency.

There are as many as 14 chapters — the first 4 deals with the underground Naga activities, *modus operandi* and so on. The author has also studied the traditional political institutions and their introduction into modern democratic system in the other chapters. Interesting chapters on the formation of the Revolutionary Government of Nagaland and the crucial problems that follow including the signing of the famous

Shillong Accord 1975, have been analysed. The Postscript on the National Socialist Council of Nagaland (NSCN) makes a critical assessment of the role of this underground outfit. Moreover, the Appendices included at the end of the book enrich the information about the Naga problem in general and insurgency in particular. Even if one is not much interested in the analytical framework provided by the author in the main chapters, but one finds immense resource materials for further analysis of the problem as contained in the Appendices which cover agreements, memoranda, constitution of the Federal Government (Nagaland), Manifesto of the NSCN, etc.

VII. Tripura

Like Manipur, Tripura was earlier a princely State. After India's independence, it became one of the Union Territories and following the reorganisation of Assam in 1971, it was established as a full-fledged State in 1972. Thus, Tripura has a long political and administrative history. Most of the books under review (1970–90), examined and analysed this long period of political, administrative and constitutional development of the State. Many Acts, Rules and Regulations were passed from time to time right from the British period of administration regarding the administration of Tripura. Tripura had also its own kings who ruled over their people. This is one of the areas of investigation and concern of those scholars who are interested in the political history and development of the State. Tripura has experienced for a number of years the problem of turmoil, unrest and socio-political tension. This happened because of the infiltration of foreign nationals to the State from the neighbouring country. This situation has brought many unpleasant happenings in Tripura. Obviously, therefore, this problem and other issues connected with it has attracted the attention of many scholars who tried to examine and analyse the situation. The after-effect of the problem of infiltration to Tripura gives rise to such other issues like crisis of identity, ethnicity and nationality. These issues have been discussed by some authors in great detail taking Tripura as a case study. Another problem which attracts the attention of scholars on Tripura is insurgency which is till now one of the major problems faced by the people of the State. This problem gives rise to secessionist movement and the mushroom growth of insurgent groups in the State. Many scholars have therefore tried to examine and analyse the constitutional and administrative development in Tripura before and after independence, the role of political parties and the formation of Governments in the State by different political parties.

The Book *Tripura Through the Ages* (A Short History of Tripura from the earliest times to A.D. 1947) by Nalini Ranjan Roy Choudhury (1983) was first published in 1977. The present volume is a revised and enlarged edition. As the title suggests the book takes a historical approach in understanding the problems of the State. The historical accounts presented in the book give us the ancient, medieval and modern periods of the history of the State. The book however may be of help to understand the political activities and development in the State as two main chapters are included on the growth of political consciousness and administrative system in Tripura. These two chapters bring out the various political movements that took place in Tripura as well as the administrative systems in the ancient, medieval and modern period.

The book *Tripura: The Land and Its People* (Ed.) Jagadis Gan-Chaudhuri (1980), as the Editor himself claims 'is more like an anthology than a compendium. It seeks to make available to the interested persons some information and materials necessary both for first-hand knowledge and for deeper understanding'. The book consists, among others, three topics on political issues — one, on the Electoral System, the other, on Local Government and another one, on Tripuri Political Consciousness. All these three essays were written by the Editor himself. The author attempts in these papers to highlight the political development as well as political consciousness among the people of Tripura. This book will be of help to students of Political Science interested in the politics and political development of Tripura.

Prodip Nath Bhattacharjee's book *The Jamatiya of Tripura* (1983) is an account of the social, religious and political activities of a section of the indigenous people of Tripura. The book is more of a sociological treatise of some Jamatiya villages to show the changes that have come over their economic, social and political life in recent years. The book is mainly based on the primary data collected by the author during a short span of time. Chapter III of the book may be of interest to students of Political Science as it deals with the political life of the people at the level of traditional village councils. Students and researchers interested in the study of such traditional village institutions at the grassroot level may find the book to be of some help.

The Riangs of Tripura by Jagadis Gan Chaudhuri (1983) is an account of the socio-economic, religious and political life of one of the tribes of Tripura, the Riangs. The book is more of a sociological study of the section (the Riangs) of the indigenous people of the State of Tripura. The last chapter (Chapter VI) of the book deals with Administration and Politics. This chapter may be of interest to students of Political Science as it describes the composition and functions of the traditional village council. This chapter provides some information on the working of such a council at the grassroot level. Students and researchers interested in finding out some basic information on traditional institutions may find the last chapter to be of some help.

The book *Tribal Insurrection in Tripura: A Study in Relative Deprivation* by Kamalini Ghosh (1984) attempts to search the roots of alienation among the tribals in Tripura and the socio-economic reasons for this phenomenon. The crisis of identity experienced by the tribals of Tripura, the quest for re-assessing their status and position in the society and the ways adopted by them to realise their goals have been the major concern of this book. The author also examines the policies and programmes adopted by the State and Union Government to contain the process of deprivation and alienation. Against this background, the book consists chapters like — Search for the Root and Parting of Ways; Liberation Here and Now; Impatience wih the democratic process and Prospects of Extremism: An Analytical evaluation. The book provides information to the understanding of the long agitation among the indigenous people of Tripura who have been pushed to the walls and fight back for survival.

The edited volume *Tribes of Tripura: A Historical Survey* (Ed.) Sudhanshu Bikash Saha (1986) contains a number of articles on different aspects and issues regarding the people of Tripura. Some articles on political activities and movements that took place among the people of the State may be of interest to students of Political Science. Articles like — Evolution and Activities of the Gana Mukti Parishad, State Congress and People's participation, Communist Movement and its influence among the tribals, Tribal Chief and his people, Tribals of Tripura and the R.S.P., Praja Mandal: Its activities among the tribals, may be of some help to understand the political scenario in Tripura. These articles provide some background materials which of course need more analytical study.

Tribal Insurgency in Tripura (A study in exploration of causes) by S.R. Bhattacharjee (1989) is another book on insurgency in N.E. India, with special reference to Tripura. Tripura is one of the insurgent-prone States of N.E. India and the book on this issue is a welcome one to understand yet another aspect of State level insurgency. The book provides an informed glimpse on the cause of tribal unrest in Tripura. The author who is associated with the tribal life in Tripura gives a methodical look into the society to find out the factors and forces — both indigenous and alien — that contributed to such unrest in the context of inbuilt inequalites in the distribution of society's wealth in the social conditions of the State in the remote past. He discusses in detail the features of insurgency in the State and also suggests some remedial measures to eliminate its causes after identifying some problems in which counter-insurgency confronts. The book contains besides historcal background on the land and people, social, cultural and economic life, two interesting chapters — one on the Political and Adminstrative Organisations and Chronology of Development of Tribal Movement and secondly, the Features of the Insurgency (in Tripura) and Concluding Remarks. The role of Tripura National Volunteers (TNV) both as an underground outfit and as an ally of the Congress in forming the coalition government is also an interesting analysis made by the author. The text of the Memorandum of Understanding with TNV is also given in the Appendix.

VIII. Journals

Some Journals which have been published from North-East India appeared in the scene from time to time. These Journals are owned, managed and published either by well-eastablished research organisations, private individuals or University Departments and others. It may, however, be noted that some such Journals which were owned and managed by private individuals did not survive long due to many reasons.

Many of the Journals aimed to devote to Social Science research pertaining mostly to serving the North-Eastern region. They also aimed to providing information, documentation and objective analysis regarding the social, cultural, economic, political and demographic problems with special reference to the problems faced by the tribal people and other ethnic communities or groups of North-East India. Some of these Journals, did try to reflect in their publications most of their lofty aims and objectives. A perusal of the issues that had been published from time to time (within the framework of the review of this survey) shows that these Journals did contribute and add certain information on different aspects of the political situations, problems and issues of North East India. However, it is not out of place to mention here that certain common political problems and issues confronting the North-Eastern region have appeared in almost all the Journals. Besides, those articles which tried to analyse the common political aspects of North-East India, case studies of the different political units of the region have also been discussed. Another common feature is the publication of book reviews in many Journals along with the general articles. The contribution made by these Journals to our understanding of the political issues in North-East India cannot however be overlooked. They did enrich and form another source of literature on Political Science as a popular discipline among the students and scholars of North-East India.

The North-Eastern Hill University has set up and published its own Journals, entitled *The NEHU Journal of Social Science and Humanities* (NEHU Publications). This Journal was published for the last many years. Going through the various volumes of the Journal, published from time to time, it was found that several articles relating to and dealing with many political aspects and issues concerning North-East India have appeared in the Journal. Certain issues of the Journal chose a specific theme and selective papers were published, e.g. Vol. II, No. 3, July–September, 1984, published two thought provoking papers on State Formation — one on the Dimasa State by J.B. Bhattacharjee and the other on Jaintia State by B. Pakem. Over and above the selective theme, different authors had contributed a number of papers in the Journal which have direct relations with the discipline of Political Science like — Autonomous District Council in certain North-Eastern States, electoral behaviour, election studies concerning Parliament, State Legislative Assemblies and District Councils. Few of the papers discussed the problem of insurgency in N.E. India — politics, middle class, nationality and ethnic identity questions etc. The History Department of NEHU has made it a point of publishing the Abstracts of Ph.D. theses submitted by its students from time to time in the Journal. Though historical in their approach, the materials that emerged out of these Abstracts can also be said to have enriched even the discipline of Political Science.

The North-East India Council for Social Science Research, Shillong, is one of the pioneering research organisations promoting and coordinating Social Science Research in all the seven States of N.E. India. It was set up on 30th June, 1974. The Council has its own Journal entitled — *Journal of North East India Council for Social Science Research*, published bi-annually. The first issue came out in April, 1977. Since then, the Council regularly published its Journal till date. Going through the various issues and articles published in the Journal during the last thirteen years (1977–90), it was found that the Council through its Journal has really covered a wide spectrum of social, economic, historical and political problems and issues concerning N.E. India. As far as literature on Political Science is concerned, many political issues were discussed by different authors from time to time. Articles on polity/state formation, traditional socio-political institutions, electoral behaviour/politics, elections to Parliament, Legislative Assemblies and Autonomous District Councils have found their due place in the Journal. Besides these, other articles like National and regional political parties, rural elite, middle class, political movements; Nationality question and ethnic identity crises, urban politics, insurgency, politics of land reforms, socio-political movements and a host of other political issues were discussed covering the whole of N.E. India. Against this background, it can be said that the Journal has really served the region's interests in diverse political studies. This Journal of NEICSSR can therefore be said, once again, to have enriched the discipline of Political Science in varied ways.

The Journal *North-East Quarterly: A Journal of Social Science Research* which appeared in the 1980s was owned and managed by few private individuals. The Journal was devoted to Social Science research pertaining chiefly to North-Eastern region. It aims at providing information, documentation and objective analysis regarding the social, economic, political and demographic problems with a focus on the peculiar nature of the problems facing the tribal people and other ethnic communities and groups of N.E. India. A perusal of the issues that had been published from time to time, shows that certain political problems relating to N.E. India were discussed by different contributors through their articles. This can be deduced into such problem and issues like — political parties (both national and regional), nationality and ethnic identity questions, regional development with special reference to NEC, agrarian politics, students movements in Assam, the Assam movement against foreign nationals, peasant movement, middle class, etc. In addition to the articles, book reviews also appeared in all the issues of the Journal. The articles that appeared from time to time did provide information and objective analysis of the political situation in N.E. India. It is however sad to say that this journal is no more in circulation. This is the general fate of many such journals from the region which are owned and managed by private individuals.

The ICSSR, North-Eastern Regional Centre, Shillong, at some point of time published its own Journal, entitled, *Journal of Social Sciences* (Bi-annual). In its March, 1981 issue (perhaps this was the only issue that came out) there are two articles which have direct relevance to the discipline of Political Science. One of them is entitled 'Social Movements, National Crisis and Social Change: The Indian Situation' by T.K. Oomen and the other 'Administration and Politics in the Framework of Development in India' by C.N. Bhalerao. Although these two articles do not have direct link with the N.E. situation, the theoretical background provided by them can be beneficial to students of the discipline to apply them to the North-East situation.

Proceedings of the North East India History Association

The North East India History Association has published its first Proceedings in 1980. Since then, these Proceedings came out regularly every year and the same have been made available to the members of the Association before the next session of the Association. Though majority of the papers published in the Proceedings have a historical approach, some articles do have a bearing and contribution to Political Science literature as well. As stated in the Introduction of this report, most of the problems/issues in N.E. India cannot be approached solely from the point of view of one particular discipline only. This is due to the fact of the nature of the problems/issues facing N.E. India. What is felt in academic circle of the scholars of the region, is the need to have an inter-disciplinary approach so that those problems/issues faced by the region can be better understood. This is true in many respects when we glanced through those papers published in the *NEIHA Proceedings* (1980–1990). Many papers are found to have direct bearing on the discipline of Political Science and thus enriched the literature on political studies relating to North-East India. Some of these papers have also been contributed by political scientists of the region themselves.

A closer examination of these papers contributed by different authors since the first issue of the Proceedings (1980), shows that a wide spectrum of issues have been discussed and covered. Some of the issues concerning N.E. India which have appeared in these Proceedings within the period of our review (1970–1990) may be broadly classified into the following categories of issues:

(i) Traditional polity/traditional socio-political institutions among different tribes of N.E. India.

(ii) Traditional and modern administration of justice.
(iii) Polity formation among some of the earlier kingdoms like Cachar, Dimasa, Kachari, Khasi, Jaintia, Ahom, etc.
(iv) Politico-cultural contacts between Assam (composite) and neighbouring areas outside N.E. India.
(v) Contact with the British: Annexation and administration and its impacts/effects on the people.
(vi) British relations with the people of N.E. India, with particular reference to the hill people.
(vii) Political Agencies/Revenue and District administration.
(viii) National, Regional and sub-national movements.
(ix) Nationality Question/Ethnic identity/Middle class/Elite among the hill societies.
(x) Nationalism and Regionalism.
(xi) Autonomous District Council/State formation/Women and Politics.
(xii) Land relations/land tenure system.

The above classification is very broad in nature. Many of the issues mentioned above have direct bearings with the politics of the North-Eastern region and the discipline of Political Science. The analysis of the varied political issues in N.E. India through these papers have really enriched our understanding of the political situation. Students of Political Science can really benefit from these indispensable sources by making use of the NEIHA Proceedings.

North-Eastern Affairs, edited by Mrs. S. Sarin, was one of the Journals published from Shillong in the 1970s. It was owned and managed by private individuals. During those years when it was in circulation, it became quite popular among the academicians and the public in general. The Journal covered a number of thought-provoking articles, mainly on the North-East problems and issues — relating to political, social, economic, demographic, etc. Besides the general problems and issues concerning North-East India, there had been series of articles based on case studies of the different political units of the region. This makes it more interesting. There were articles which discussed about the current political events that took place in the different States of North-East India during those years. Articles on traditional chiefs and socio-political institutions, political parties (national and regional), freedom/statehood movements, insurgency, nationality question, ethnic identity crisis, etc. had appeared in different issues of the Journal from time to time. These articles have therefore contributed a lot to our understanding of the political situation in North-East India during the 1970s and 1980s. However, as was the case with other Journals owned and managed by private individuals, this one also has unfortunately ceased its publication.

Social Research is a quarterly Journal of the Institute of Social Research, Shillong. It is a forum formed by private individuals to promote research. This forum published research findings, theory and critical analysis in Social Sciences. Since the early 1980s, it published articles in all branches of Social Science pertaining to any region of India especially the North-East. A closer examination of the articles published through this Journal since the early 1980s, shows that these articles cover a wide range of issues and problems pertaining to political situation in N.E. India. Broadly speaking, issues and problems like International relations between the States of N.E. India with the neighbouring countries like Burma (Myanmar), Nepal, Bangladesh, etc., Muslim League politics and movement in Assam, ethnic identity — problem and crisis, British policy towards N.E. India, State Politics, Regional Political Parties and Regionalism, Electoral Studies, Tribal economy and development, Traditional institution/chiefs among the tribals of N.E. India. As in the case of other privately owned Journals, this one also is no longer in circulation.

North-Eastern Spectrum was a monthly Journal published from Guwahati from 1976 onwards. It published articles on social, political, economic, demgraphic, anthropological problems and issues, etc. covering the seven States of North-East India, North Bengal and Sikkim. Besides regular monthly articles by various authors, it also published News Letters from the North-Eastern States and book reviews. This monthly Journal had been able to cover extensively the various problems and issues faced by the States mentioned above. Some of the articles published from time to time discussed a number of political issues and problems of the North-Eastern region in partiular. Students of Political Science will benefit from those articles relating to the discipline. Added to this, are the News Letters relating to the current happenings in the North-Eastern States which now form part of the basic information on what had happened earlier. The various issues of the Journal form an important source of information. However, it is unfortunate to see that this Journal has also met the same fate like others, because its publication has already ceased and it is no more in circulation now.

Bibliography

Anand, V.K. *Conflict in Nagaland (A study of Insurgency and Counter-Insurgency)*, Chanakya Publications, Delhi, 1980.

Assam Sahitya Sabha. *Eclipse in the East: An Analysis of the Present Agitation in Assam* (2nd edition), Gauhati, 1980.

Bareh, Hamlet. *The History and Culture of the Khasi People*, Spectrum Publications, Guwahati, 1985 (2nd revised & enlarged edition).

Bareh, Hamlet (Ed.). *Gazetteer of India, Nagaland (Kohima District)*, Government of Nagaland, 1970.

Bareh, Hamlet. *Meghalaya*, North-Eastern India News and Feature Service, Shillong, 1974.

Barpujari, H.K. *Problem of the Hill Tribes: N.E. Frontier (1822–1842)*, Vol. I, Lawyers' Book Stall, Gauhati, 1970.

Barpujari, H.K. *Problem of the Hill Tribes: N.E. Frontier (1843–1872)*, United Publishers, Gauhati, 1978.

Barpujari, H.K. *Assam in the Days of the Company (1826–1858)*, Spectrum Publications, Gauhati, 1980.

Barpujari, H.K. *Problem of the Hill Tribes: N.E. Frontier (1873–1962)*, Vol. III, Spectrum Publications, Gauhati 1981.

Barpujari, H.K. *An Account of Assam and her Administration (1603–1822 A.D.)*, Spectrum Publications, Gauhati, 1988.

Barooah, Nirode K. *David Scott in North-East India (1802–1831): A Study in British Paternalism*, Munshiram Manoharlal, New Delhi, 1970.

Bandyopadhyay, P.K. *Leadership Among the Mizos: An Emerging Dimension*, B.R. Publishing Corporation, Delhi, 1985.

Baveja, J.D. *The Land Where the Bamboo Flowers*, Publication Board Assam Gauhati, 1970.

Bhat, Sudhakar. *The Challenge of the North-East*, Popular Prakashan, Bombay, 1975.

Bhattacharjya, Umasaday. *Local Government in Khasi Hills*, Vivek Publishing Company, Delhi, 1980.

Bhattacharjee, J.B. (Ed). *Social Tension in North-East India*, Researcdh India Publications, Calcutta, 1982.

Bhattacharjee, Pradip Nath. *The Jamatiyas of Tripura*, Directorate of Research, Government of Tripura, 1983.

Bhattacharjee, Debasish. *Bureaucracy and Development in Meghalaya*, Uppal Publishing House, New Delhi, 1986.

Bhattacharjee, J.B. (Ed). *Sequence of Development in North-East India: A Study in Tradition, Continuity and Change*, Omsons Publications, 1989.

Bhattacharjee, S.R. *Tribal Insurgency in Tripura: A Study in Exploration of Causes*, Inter-India Publications, New Delhi, 1989.

Bose, Manilal. *Historical and Constitutional Documents of North-Eastern India (1824–1973)*, Concept Publishing Company, New Delhi, 1979.

Bose, Manilal. *British Policy in the NEFA*, Concept Publishing Company, New Delhi, 1979.

Bose, M.L. *Development of Administration in Assam*, Concept Publishing Company, New Delhi, 1985.

Bose, T.C. (Ed.) *Political Development in North-East India* (in two volumes), Political Science Department, Dibrugarh University, 1976 & 1978.

Cantlie, Sir Keith. *Notes on Khasi Law*, (Ed. & Rep.) A.S. Khongphai, Shillong, 1974.

Chakravorty, B. Ch. *British Relations with the Hill Tribes of Assam Since 1858*, Firma KLM Pvt. Ltd., Calcutta, 1981.

Chatterji, N. *Zawlbuk As a Social Institution in the Mizo Society*, Tribal Research Institute, Aizawl, 1975.

Chatterjee, Suhas. *Mizoram Encyclopaedia* (in three volumes), Jaico Publishing House, Delhi, 1990.

Chaube, S.K. *Hill Politics in North-East India*, Orient Longman, Calcutta, 1973.

Chaube, S.K. *Electoral Politics in North-East India*, Universities Press, Madras, 1985.

Chattopadhyay, S.K. (Ed). *Tribal Institutions of Meghalaya*, Spectrum Publications, Guwahati, 1985.

Chattopadhyay, S.K. (Ed). *The Jaintias: Socio-Political Institutions of Jaintia Hills*, Cosmo Publications, New Delhi, 1988.

Chattopadhya, S.K. & Sangma, M.S. (Eds.). *The Garo Customary Laws*, Directorate of Arts & Culture, Government of Meghalaya, Shillong, 1989.

Chaudhuri, J. Gan. *The Riangs of Tripura*, Directorate of Research, Government of Tripura, 1983.

Chaudhuri, J. Gan. *Tripura: The Land and Its People*, Leeladevi Publications, Delhi, 1980.

Chaudhuri, K.C. *North-Eastern India: The Problem and Its Solution*, Abhoy Ashram Birati, Calcutta, 1980.

Chowdhury, J.N. *Arunanchal Panorama: A Study in Profile*, Author, 1973.

Chowdhury, J.N. *The Khasi Canvas*, Jaya Chowdhury, Shillong, 1978.

Chowdhury, J.N. *Arunachal Through the Ages*, Jaya Chowdhury, Shillong, 1982.

Compiled by Authority. *Provincial Gazetteer of Assam*, Cultural Publishing House, Delhi, 1983 (Reprint).

Das, S.K. *Spotlight on Assam*, Premier Book Service, Chanderdur, Maharashtra, 1989.

Datta, P.S. (Ed.) *Ethnic Movements in Poly-Cultural Assam*, Har-Anand Publications, New Delhi, 1990.

Deka, K.M. (Ed.) *Nationalism and Regionalism in North-East India*, Dibrugarh University, 1985.

Dev, Bimal J. & Lahiri, Dilip K. *Assam Muslims: Politics and Cohesion*, Mittal Publications, Delhi, 1985.

Dev, Bimal J. & Lahiri, Dilip K. *Manipur: Culture and Politics*, Mittal Publications, Delhi, 1987.

Dewan Vijay K. *Assam Issue: The Beginning — The End and The Beginning*, Author, 1985.

Dunbar, George. *Frontiers*, Omsons Publications, New Delhi, 1984 (Reprint).

Dutta, P.N. *Impact of the West on the Khasis and Jaintias: A Survey of Political, Economic and Social Changes*, Cosmo Publications, New Delhi, 1982.

Gangmumei, Kabui. *Anal: A Transborder Tribe of Manipur*, Mittal Publications, Delhi, 1985.

Gangopadhyaya, D.K. (Compiled and edited). *Revenue Administration in Assam, Government of Assam*, 1990.

Ghosh, B.B. *History of Nagaland*, S. Chand and Company Ltd. New Delhi, 1982.

Ghosh, Kamalini. *Tribal Insurrection in Tripura: A Study in Relative Deprivation*, Booklinks Corporation, Hyderabad, 1984.

Giri, Helen. *The Khasis Under British Rule (1824–1947)*, Akashi Book Depot, Shillong, 1990.

Gohain, Hirendra Nath. *Assam: A Burning Question*, Spectrum Publications, Guwahati, 1985.

Goswami, S.K. *A History of Revenue Administration in Assam (1228–1826 A.D.)*, Spectrum Publications, Guwahati, 1986.

Goswami, Shrutidev. *Aspects of Revenue Administration in Assam (1826–1874)*, Mittal Publications, Delhi, 1987.

Gupta, Shekhar. *Assam: A Valley Divided*, Vikas Publishing House Pvt. Ltd., New Delhi, 1984.

Hansaria, B.L. *Sixth Schedule to the Constitution of India: A Study*, Gita Hansaria, Gauhati, 1983.

Hidayatullah, M. *The Fifth and Sixth Schedules to the Constitution of India*, Ashok Publishing House, Gauhati, 1979.

Hluna, John Vanlal. *Church and Political Upheaval in Mizoram*, Mizo History Association, Aizawl, 1985.

Horam, M. *Naga Polity*, B.R. Publishing Corporation, Delhi, 1975.

Horam, M. *Naga Insurgency: The Last Thirty Years*, Cosmo Publications, New Delhi, 1988.

Horam, M. *North-East India: A Profile*, Cosmo Publications, New Delhi, 1990.

Hunter, W.W. *A Statistical Account of Assam* (Vol. II), B.R. Publishing Corporation, Delhi, 1975 (Reprint).

Kar, P.C. *British Annexation of Garo Hills*, Nababharat Publishers, Calcutta, 1970.

Kar, M. *Muslims in Assam Politics*, Omsons Publications, 1990.

Kamkhenthang, H., Vaiphei, S.P. *et al. In Search of Identity*, Kuki-Chin Baptist Mission, Imphal, 1986.

Khongphai, A.S. *Principles of Khasi Law*, Author, Shillong, 1974.

Kusum & Bakshi, P.M. *Customary Law and Justice in the Tribal Areas of Meghalaya*, N.M. Tripathi Pvt. Ltd., Bombay, 1982.

Kyndiah, P.R. *Meghalaya: Yesterday and Today*, Har-Anand Publications, 1990.

Luthra, P.N. *Nagaland: From a District to a State*, M.P. Hazarika, Director of Information and Public Relations, Arunachal Pradesh, Shillong, 1974.

Mackenzie, Alexander. *The North-East Frontier of India*, Mittal Publications, New Delhi, 1979 (Reprint).

Mali, D.D. *Revenue Administration in Assam*, Omsons Publications, Gauhati, 1985.

Medhi, Kunja. *State Politics in India: A Study of Assam Legislative Assembly*, Omsons Publications, Gauhati, 1988.

Misra, Udayon. *North-East India: Quest for Identity*, Omsons Publications, Guwahati, 1988.

Moffat Mills, A.J. *Report of Assam*, Gian Publications, Delhi, 1980 (Reprint).

Mohanta, Bijan. *Administrative Development of Arunachal Pradesh (1875–1975)*, Uppal Publishing House, New Delhi, 1984.

Murty, T.S. *Assam: The Difficult Years (A Study of Political Development in 1979–83)*, Himalayan Books, New Delhi, 1983.

Nag, Amit Kr. *The Mizo Dilemma*, Tribal Mirror Publications, Silchar, 1984.

Nag, Sajal. *Roots of Ethnic Conflict: Nationality Question in North-East India*, Manohar, Delhi, 1990.

Nibedon, Nirmal. *Mizoram: The Dagger Brigade*, Lancers Publishers, New Delhi, 1980.

Pakem, B. (Ed.). *Shillong 1971–1981*, Research India Publications, Calcutta, 1984..

Pakem, B. (Ed.). *Nationality, Ethnicity and Cultural Identity in North-East India*, Omsons Publications, Guwahati, 1990.

Parry, N.E. *A Monograph on Lushai Customs and Ceremonies*, Firma KLM Pvt. Ltd., Calcutta, 1976 (Reprint).

Paul, Madan, C. *Dimensions of Tribal Movements in India — A Study of Udayachal in Assam Valley*, Inter-India Publications, New Delhi, 1989.

Phukon, Girin. *Assam Attitude to Federalism*, Sterling Publishers Pvt. Ltd., 194.

Prasad, R.N. *Government and Politics in Mizoram (1947–1986)*, Northern Book Centre, New Delhi, 1987.

Rafiabadi, H.N. *Assam: From Agitation to Accord*, Genuine Publications & Media Pvt. Ltd., New Delhi, 1988.

Rao, V. Venkata. *A Century of Tribal Politics in North-East India (1874–1974)*, Vol. I, Assam (1874–1980), S. Chand and Company Ltd., New Delhi, 1983.

Rao, V. Venkata, Pakem, B. & Hazarika, N. *A Century of Government and Politics in North-East India*, Vol. II, Meghalaya (1874–1983), S. Chand and Company Ltd, New Delhi, 1984.

Rao, V. Venkata, Thansanga, H. & Hazarika, N. *A Century of Government and Politics in North-East India*, Vol. III, Mizoram, S. Chand and Company Ltd., New Delhi, 1987.

Ray, B. Datta (Ed.). *Electoral Politics in Meghalaya* NEICSSR, Shillong, 1978.

Ray, B. Datta (Ed). *The Emergence and Role of Middle Class in North-East India*, Uppal Publishing House, New Delhi, 1982.

Ray, B. Datta. *Tribal Identity and Social Tension in North-East India*, Omsons Publications, Guwahati, 1989.

Ray, Animesh. *Mizoram: Dynamics of Change*, Pearl Publishers, Calcutta, 1982.

Reid, Sir Robert. *The Lushai Hills*, Firma KLM Pvt. Ltd., Calcutta, 1978 (Reprint).

Report on the Administration of North-East India (1921–22), Mittal Publications, Delhi, 1984 (Reprint).

Robinson, William. *A Descriptive Account of Assam*, Sanskaran Prakashak, Delhi, 1975 (Reprint).

Roy Choudhury, N.R. *Tripura Through the Ages (A Short History of Tripura from the Earliest Times to 1947 AD)*, Sterling Publishers Pvt. Ltd., 1983.

Rustomji, Nari. *Imperilled Frontiers (India's North-Eastern Borderlands)*, OUP, 1983.

Saha, S. Bikash (Ed). *Tribes of Tripura: A Historical Survey*, Rupali Book Store, Agartala, 1986.

Sanjayya. *Assam: A Crisis of Identity*, Spectrum Publications, Gauhati, 1980.

Sareen, H.K. *Insurgency in North-East India (A Study of the Sino-American Role)*, Sterling Publishers Pvt. Ltd., New Delhi, 1980.

Sarin, V.I.K. *India's North-East in Flames*, Vikas Publishing House Pvt. Ltd., New Delh, 1980.

Sarkar, Jayanta & Ray, B. Datta (Eds.). *Social and Political Institutions of the Hill People of North-East India*, Director General, A.S.I., Govt. of India, 1990.

Sarma, A.C. *Tai Ahom System of Administration*, B.R. Publishing Corporation, Delhi, 1996.

Sema, Hokishe. *Emergence of Nagaland: Socio-Economic and Political Transformation and the Future,* Vikas Publishing House Pvt. Ltd., Delhi, 1986.

Sen Gupta, Kollol. *Without Roots (Part I & II),* Bimal Sen Gupta, Shillong, 1979.

Sen, Soumen. *Between Tradition and Change (A Perspective of Meghalaya),* B.R. Publishing Corporation, Delhi, 1988.

Shadap-Sen, N.C. *The Origin and Early History of the Khasi-Synteng People,* Firma KLM Pvt. Ltd., Calcutta, 1981.

Sharma, Manorama. *Social and Economic Change in Assam: Middle Class Hegemony,* Ajanta Publications, Delhi, 1990.

Singh, Kynpham. *A Collection of Writings About Khasi Hills and Khasis,* Author, Shillong, 1979.

Singh, Chandrika. *Political Evolution of Nagaland,* Lancers Publishers, New Delhi, 1981.

Singh, Bhawani. *Politics of Alienation in Assam,* Ajanta Publications, Delhi, 1984.

Singh, Ravindra P. *Electoral Politics in Manipur: A Spatio-Temporal Study,* Concept Publishing Company, New Delhi, 1981.

Singh, B.P. *The Problem of Change: A Study of North-East India,* OUP, 1987.

Sinha, Kamaleshwar. *Meghalaya: Triumph of the Tribal Genius,* Publication Division (ISSD), Delhi, 1970.

Syiemlieh, D.R. *British Administration in Meghalaya: Policy and Patterns,* Heritage Publishers, New Delhi, 1989.

Talukdar, A.C. *Political Transition in the Grassroots in Tribal India,* Omsons Publications, Guwahati, 1987.

Thanga, Lal Biak. *The Mizos: A Study in Racial Personality,* United Publishers, Gauhati, 1978.

Thangchinlian, G. & Jamkhanthang, T. *The Paite Customary Laws,* The Paite National Council, Manipur, 1986.

Woodthorpe, R.G. *The Lushai Expedition (1871–1872),* Spectrum Publications, Gauhati, 1980 (Reprint).

Yonuo, Asoso. *The Rising Nagas: A Historical and Political Study,* Vivek Publishing House, Delhi, 1974.

Yonuo, Asoso. *Nagas Struggle Against the British Rule Under Jadonang and Rani Gaidinliu (1925–1947),* Leno Printing Press, Kohima, 1982.

Journals

- The NEHU Journal of Social Sciences and Humanities.
- Journal of North-East India Council for Social Science Research.
- North-East Quarterly: A Journal of Social Science Research.
- Journal of Social Sciences (NERC-ICSSR).
- Proceedings of the North-East India History Association.
- North-Eastern Affairs.
- Social Research.
- North-Eastern Spectrum.